China and the Bomb

This book has been written
under the auspices of
The Center for International Affairs
and
The East Asian Research Center
Harvard University

CHINA
AND THE
BOMB

MORTON H. HALPERIN

FREDERICK A. PRAEGER, *Publishers*
New York • Washington • London

FREDERICK A. PRAEGER, *Publishers*
111 Fourth Avenue, New York 3, N.Y., U.S.A.
77–79 Charlotte Street, London W.1, England

Published in the United States of America in 1965
by Frederick A. Praeger, Inc., Publishers

Library of Congress Catalog Card Number: 65–15646

Printed in the United States of America

To INA

Foreword

THIS BOOK WAS BEGUN AS A monograph for the Council on Foreign Relations project on the United States and China in World Affairs. I am grateful to the Council and to Robert Blum, director of the China project, for support of my research and for permitting me to incorporate my work done for the Council into this book. I have also benefited from discussions with an advisory group set up by the Council and ably chaired by A. Doak Barnett. The Council is, of course, in no way responsible for this final product.

The Harvard East Asian Research Center, drawing on funds provided by a Department of Defense contract, has generously supported my research. It was the East Asian Center that made it possible for me to undertake a trip to the Far East. I am especially grateful to its Associate Director, John Lindbeck, for urging me to begin working in the field of

Chinese military policy and for providing constant encouragement.

It is also a pleasure to acknowledge my continuing debt to the Harvard Center for International Affairs for intellectual stimulation and financial assistance.

The writing of much of this book took place while I was Visiting Lecturer in Strategic Studies at the University of London. I am grateful to Professor Michael Howard of the Department of War Studies for the invitation that brought me to London and to the Rockefeller Foundation for a grant in international relations that made my stay possible.

Various observations made about preceding drafts of my manuscript, both in writing and during discussion sessions at the Council on Foreign Relations, were quite helpful. I have benefited from comments by: Hanson W. Baldwin, A. Doak Barnett, James P. Baxter, 3rd, Robert Blum, Lawrence S. Finkelstein, Fred Greene, Robert M. Ginsburgh, A. M. Halpern, Harold C. Hinton, Amos A. Jordan, Jr., William W. Kaufmann, Paul Kreisberg, William P. Maddox, Marshall E. Sanders, Thomas C. Schelling, Warner Schilling, and Richard A. Yudkin.

The manuscript of *China and the Bomb* was originally completed prior to the Chinese nuclear detonation in October, 1964. I have substantially revised, rewritten, and updated it since then. My wife has again combined her roles of research assistant, critic, and editor with those of wife and mother. Mark Evan Halperin arrived today; it is sobering to realize that the distant future discussed in this book will be history before his generation comes to grips with these problems.

MORTON H. HALPERIN

Cambridge, Massachusetts
January 11, 1965

Contents

China and the Bomb

1

Force and Restraint
in the Sino-American
Confrontation

THE RELATIONSHIP BETWEEN
the People's Republic of China and the United States has
been one of hostility and mutual suspicion from the time of
the establishment of a Communist state in China. Although the
United States was active during and following World War II in
trying to bring about a coalition regime on the Chinese mainland, there was never any doubt in the minds of either Chinese
Communist or American officials that American sympathies
lay with the Kuomintang. When, in 1949, the Communists
captured the mainland and established the People's Republic
of China, there was little doubt that the stage had been set
for a major confrontation in the Far East. Mao Tse-tung, in
his now famous "leaning to one side" speech in July, 1949,

3

made clear his regime's adherence to the Soviet bloc and its hostility to "imperialism" in the Far East and throughout the world.[1]

Since 1949, when the two powers were already antagonistic, hostility between Communist China and the United States has if anything intensified. After the defeat of the Chinese Nationalist regime and its escape to Taiwan, American policy was, in the words of Secretary of State Dean Acheson, to "let the dust settle" before making any further moves. The United States took the position that it would not intervene to protect Taiwan but at the same time that it did not envisage early recognition of the Peking regime. Soon faced with the North Korean invasion of South Korea, however, President Truman decided to defend Taiwan—on the grounds that now that Communism in Asia had shown itself to be expansionist, it was necessary to prevent its further spread by the use of military force. The decision to put the Seventh Fleet in the Taiwan Straits (to prevent Chiang Kai-shek from moving against the mainland as well as the Chinese Communists from invading Taiwan) was taken in the opening days of the Korean War, when the pressure of other problems was such that little time could have been given to the decision.[2] In any event, with the interposing of the Seventh Fleet in the Taiwan Straits, the United States put herself directly and immediately into a serious conflict with the Chinese Communist regime. She was now intervening actively in the Chinese civil war, and she was propping up, supplying military aid to, and defending the regime that the Communists had defeated and that they thought they were within years, if not months, of wiping out. Within a few months, the armies of the United States and China clashed in Korea. Subsequently, the two

[1] "On the People's Democratic Dictatorship," *Selected Works of Mao Tse-tung* (Peking: Foreign Languages Press, 1961), IV, 411–24.

[2] On the American decision to intervene in the Taiwan Straits, see Tang Tsou, *America's Failure in China: 1941–50* (Chicago: University of Chicago Press, 1963), pp. 558–64.

countries saw themselves on opposing sides in a number of military encounters, including those on the Sino-Indian border, in Indochina, and in the Taiwan Straits. The involvement of the two countries in these and other postwar military clashes in the Far East has varied enormously—from the direct confrontation of their armed forces to the providing of diplomatic support to opposing forces. Indeed, no matter what form the engagement has taken, in every major diplomatic or military crisis in Asia since 1949, China and the United States have viewed each other as being on opposite sides. Each government refuses to recognize the other and establishes such conditions on recognition as to render it improbable—with the United States insisting upon Chinese renunciation of force in the Taiwan Straits, and China demanding the liberation of Taiwan.

Thus, in considering the implications for the United States of a Chinese nuclear capability, one is dealing with the relationship between two mutually hostile nations. It is therefore natural that the United States is concerned about *any* increase in China's military power. The acquisition of nuclear weapons, however, has been viewed by the United States as constituting a very special category of arms increase, and it is important to recognize that the United States would be opposed to and concerned about the Chinese detonation of a nuclear device and the Chinese development of a nuclear capability no matter whether China were neutral or, indeed, allied to the United States. In a speech at Ann Arbor, Michigan, in June, 1962, Secretary of Defense Robert S. McNamara plainly stated the American opposition to the spread of national nuclear capabilities even among American allies:

> Relatively weak national nuclear forces with enemy cities as their targets are not likely to be sufficient to perform even the function of deterrence. If they are small, and perhaps vulnerable on the ground or in the air, or inaccurate, a major antagonist can take a variety of measures to counter them. Indeed,

if a major antagonist came to believe that there was a substantial likelihood of it being used independently, this force would be inviting a pre-emptive first strike against it. In the event of war, the use of such a force against the cities of a major nuclear power would be tantamount to suicide, whereas its employment against significant military targets would have a negligible effect on the outcome of the conflict. Meanwhile, *the creation of a single additional national nuclear force encourages a proliferation of nuclear powers with all of its attendant dangers.*

In short, then, limited nuclear capabilities, operating independently, are dangerous, expensive, prone to obsolescence, and lacking in credibility as a deterrent. [Italics added.]

One of the arguments supporting the American opposition to any national nuclear force is that the creation of each such force makes it more likely that others will be developed and that a substantial proliferation of nuclear weapons will follow. This argument against the general spread of nuclear weapons had frequently been made in both the declarations and the actions of American officials prior to the Chinese nuclear detonation on October 16, 1964, and it was restated by President Johnson and other officials following the detonation.[3] In opposing the spread of nuclear weapons, the United States has been motivated by a feeling that the control over nuclear weapons by additional countries would make the world a more dangerous one and one in which the power of the United States was reduced. The Soviet Union's development of a nuclear capability substantially reduced American security and power; the further spread of nuclear power to Britain

[3] It is true that the American program for a sharing of atomic power may be seen as an exception to this general policy, in that it has had the effect of spreading nuclear technology throughout the world. But that effect is inadvertent. The United States has demanded safeguards that have prevented the direct application of the reactors it supplies to other countries to military ends, and in general it has tended vastly to overestimate the peacetime value of atomic energy, particularly as a source of electric power. See Arnold Kramish, *The Peaceful Atom in Foreign Policy* (New York: Harper & Bros., for the Council on Foreign Relations, 1953).

and France does not appear to have been in the American interest; the acquisition of nuclear weapons by other, less stable, and more expansionist countries threatens to increase the dangers facing the United States and the whole world.

Local arms races for nuclear weapons between countries hostile to each other are likely to be extremely volatile, and could lead to the danger of their preventive use by the country first obtaining them. Even if this did not occur, it appears that over the long run, the more countries that have nuclear weapons, the more likely it is that nuclear weapons will be used. This is less a matter of statistics than a consequence of the fact that the nations now possessing nuclear weapons tend to be responsible and experienced in the matter of nuclear power, and to be in the position where they are deterred from using that power because they recognize the great destruction it would bring. Smaller, less experienced powers are more prone to use force to settle their disputes. They would be more likely to use nuclear weapons in the event of war since their very existence as independent states may be at issue. The local use of nuclear weapons would be a major disaster which the United States would want to prevent not only for its own sake but even more because *any* use of nuclear weapons raises the grave possibility of a major nuclear war. The proliferation of nuclear weapons among a few lesser powers therefore could set off a chain that would make the use of nuclear weapons more likely on one or several occasions and that would significantly increase the likelihood of general nuclear war.

Thus, the United States has refused to aid any country, whether ally or neutral, in the development of a national nuclear-weapons force with the exception of the special agreement with Great Britain. Under the Kennedy and Johnson administrations, the government has apparently tried to convince both Great Britain and France to abandon their national nuclear programs and has sought to provide a means of their dissolution in multilateral or inter-allied nuclear forces. The United States has also encouraged other nations in Europe, the Far East, and the Middle East not to develop nuclear weapons.

There is no doubt that the United States would be giving this sort of advice to a friendly Chinese government, but it is also clear that the hostility of the present Peking government toward the United States makes the problem of a Chinese nuclear capability much more acute and more difficult to solve. It might even be said that a major motive for China's nuclear program is the regime's hostility to the United States and the Western bloc.

CHINESE FOREIGN-POLICY OBJECTIVES

To appreciate the danger that a Chinese nuclear capability creates for the United States, it is necessary to consider briefly the motivation and content of Chinese foreign policy, as well as the part that force has played in the implementation of that policy. This will make possible an assessment of the changes that might come should China develop a nuclear-weapons capability, and of the political and military uses to which the Chinese might be tempted to put any nuclear-weapons delivery systems they develop. It is also necessary to explore American objectives in the Far East and how they are threatened by a Chinese nuclear capability.[4]

[4] For more detailed discussion, see A. Doak Barnett, *Communist China and Asia* (New York: Harper & Bros., for the Council on Foreign Relations, 1960); and Allen S. Whiting, "Foreign Policy of Communist China," in Roy C. Macridis (ed.), *Foreign Policy in World Politics* (Englewood Cliffs, N.J.: Prentice-Hall, 1958). For a definitive history of American relations with China from Pearl Harbor to the Chinese entry in the Korean War, see Tang Tsou, *America's Failure in China*. The official statement of American policy through 1949 is the China White Paper, *United States Relations with China, with Special Reference to the Period 1944–49* (Washington, D.C.: U.S. Department of State, 1949). For the Chinese Communist viewpoint, see Edgar Snow, *The Other Side of the River: Red China Today* (New York: Random House, 1961), pp. 85–92 and *passim*. For a symposium on American viewpoints, see *China Quarterly*, No. 10 (April–June, 1962), pp. 45–83.

In trying to discover the basic motivations of Chinese foreign policy, it is useless to argue whether it is primarily "Communist" or primarily "Chinese," but important to realize that it is shaped by many historical, geopolitical, and ideological factors, as well as by domestic objectives and attitudes. History affects Chinese foreign policy both insofar as the historic national objectives of China continue to guide her in modern times and insofar as the personal historical experiences of Chinese Communist leaders have been important in shaping their world outlook and their idea of what China's position in the world should be.[5]

The Peking government is influenced by its inheritance of the mantle of leadership in a country that has considered herself the center of the world. Though no doubt rejecting the explicit notion of the "mandate from heaven," the Communist regime, as the inheritor of power in China, nevertheless feels obliged to seek to restore to China at least some of her traditional territories, including Tibet and Taiwan, and to establish Chinese hegemony in the Far East. It has likewise sought to create a position for China as a great power in the modern world. The personal historical experiences of the regime's leaders—who have remained remarkably stable over the past three decades[6]—have also been important—in establishing their belief in the validity of force as a necessary instrument in foreign policy, in inducing hostility toward the United States, and in producing a keen sense of the need for self-reliance and of the unreliability of coalitions or alliances with other groups or nations.

The Communist regime to some extent also feels the pres-

5 For a slightly different breakdown of Chinese Communist motivations, as well as for a more extensive discussion of this problem in the context of the Chinese decision to enter the Korean War, see Allen S. Whiting, *China Crosses the Yalu* (New York: Macmillan, 1960), pp. 1–13.

6 Mao Tse-tung has headed the Chinese Communist Party since the early 1930's. Most of China's present leaders participated in the Long March of 1934–35.

sures that throughout China's history have been generated by
China's geographical position. The regime has had to confront and solve a number of problems arising from the fact
that because of China's weakness in the modern period, her
power has seldom been exerted on her border areas, and
therefore that her borders have been to a large measure ill
defined or undefined. China's geographical position also makes
her fearful of foreign sea and air military powers that control
bases along her periphery. At the same time, the long border
with the Soviet Union makes her equally aware of the possibility and danger of ground attacks. The Peking regime initially attempted to deal with these dangers by establishing a
firm alliance with the Soviet Union and by concentrating its
energies on the hostile sea and air power of the United States.

But to note the foregoing points is not to deny that ideology
has to a large degree shaped Chinese foreign policy since 1949.
For the leaders' adherence to a Maoist variant of Marxism
and Leninism has affected their image of the world and how
it works.[7] In a very real sense, ideology shapes the regime's
objectives. Mao's ideological blinders, fortifying his historical
experience, helped him to arrive at the decision to ally the
Peking regime with the Soviet Union, but they probably also
caused him to overestimate the extent to which he could depend on Soviet support for another "socialist" state. The
Maoist image of the world leads the regime to accept violence
as a legitimate tool of policy and to view domestic politics
in other countries as a manifestation of the class struggle. It
was this view of politics that in the early years prompted the
regime to denigrate neutralism and to categorize the governments in India and elsewhere as neo-imperialistic regimes
under the control of Western lackeys. While this particular
dogma has in recent years become somewhat less rigid, the

---

[7] What Nathan Leites in dealing with the Soviet Union calls the "opera-
tional code." See Leites, *A Study of Bolshevism* (Glencoe, Ill.: Free Press of
Glencoe, 1953). No comparable study exists on Communist China.

Chinese continue to view domestic politics of other countries through the simplifying prism of Marxism-Leninism and, apparently, to overestimate the strength of the forces of Communist revolution. Again, Chinese hostility to the United States, aroused by historical experience, is reinforced by the ideological image of America as an imperialist and capitalist world power that is everywhere opposing the spread of Communist influence. Chinese foreign policy in areas far removed from China's borders is especially motivated by Marxist-Leninist ideological considerations—in the absence of any traditional Chinese interest in Latin America, the Middle East, or Africa. Here, the ideology of the Chinese leaders affects not only the way in which they look at the countries but also how they frame their objectives in relation to them. A Nationalist regime in China might have the same objectives concerning the actual extent of Chinese territory and conditions near her borders, but would be unlikely to be as actively interested in African, Latin American, or Middle Eastern developments.

The interrelation of domestic and foreign policy in any country is complicated, varying over time. On the one hand, it would be wrong to assume that foreign policy is simply an extension of domestic political pressures and trends, but, on the other hand, it would be equally dangerous to assume that there is no relation at all between the two. This is certainly true in Communist China. It seems clear that the primary Chinese objective in foreign affairs is to hold the territory currently under Chinese Communist control—a goal that is largely dictated by the regime's somewhat negative desire to be free to determine the policies and way of life of the area it captured in 1949. In addition, the foreign policy of China has been influenced, to some extent at least, by the more positive desire for rapid internal economic development moving toward a self-sufficient industrialized economy. Clearly, this second desire has not always been the dominant one; it appears, in fact, to be seriously weakened by the current dispute with the Soviet Union.

Considered in terms of objectives rather than motivations, the Peking regime has had a hierarchy of territorial objectives, the first being to maintain the area currently under Communist control, and the second being to fill out the borders of China. In the case of Tibet, China could and did expand her boundaries without jeopardizing the home territory, but in the Taiwan Straits, where there was and is a conflict, priority has been given to the security of present Chinese Communist territory. Beyond the maintenance of control over traditional Chinese territory, the Peking regime seems to be interested in the first instance in having friendly neutral nations on its periphery—countries that would not accept American military bases on their soil and that would in general accept Communist China's lead in foreign policy. In a longer perspective, the Chinese appear to be interested in the establishment of Communist regimes throughout the world as well as on their own borders.

The Peking regime has a more intangible goal as well: to establish China as one of the great powers of the world. It has sought to assert China's right to be consulted on all major international questions, in particular with reference to the Far East, as well as on questions of general disarmament. For example, China both served her national interest and bid for international status when she openly accused the Soviet Union of "weakening the socialist camp" by signing a test-ban treaty with the United States. Within the Communist bloc, Peking has claimed to be equal to the Soviet Union in directing Communist parties and regimes in nations throughout the world. It has pressed for the acceptance of its more militant strategy as a basic guide for Communist parties.[8] And

---

[8] Certain aspects of the Sino-Soviet dispute as they affect the developing Chinese nuclear capability are treated in later chapters, but the general question of the Sino-Soviet dispute and its impact on Chinese foreign policy lies beyond the scope of this enquiry. Events in this area have moved almost too

the Chinese detonation of a nuclear device has reinforced its belief in the validity of these views.

THE ROLE OF FORCE IN CHINESE POLICY

The Peking regime views the relation of force to policy in terms of the Maoist doctrine that "political power grows out of the barrel of a gun."[9] Military force will be at the base of any Chinese Communist effort to implement its foreign-policy objectives, then, in that force, in the minds of the Peking leaders, is an inevitable and necessary instrument of foreign policy.

Not only in her polemics with the Soviet Union, but also in her actions, China has made clear her belief that force is an instrument of policy and that general and complete disarmament is first of all an impossible objective and, second, undesirable for propagandistic reasons because it reduces the will of the people to employ military force. The Chinese apparently make a sharp distinction, however, between their doctrines on the inevitability and desirability of employing limited military force and their attitude toward a direct military confrontation with the United States. There is nothing in Chinese Communist words or deeds to suggest that at present they welcome such confrontation. In fact, the Chinese seem to have attached the highest priority to the task of avoiding a direct military clash with the United States that could lead to a nuclear war. Even in the activities they have urged upon the Soviet Union in underdeveloped nations, they seem to

---

fast for analysis to keep pace. The history of the dispute to 1961 is to be found in Donald S. Zagoria, *The Sino-Soviet Conflict, 1956–1961* (Princeton, N.J.: Princeton University Press, 1962). Documentation of the dispute, with analysis, is to be found in G. F. Hudson *et al.* (eds.), *The Sino-Soviet Dispute* (New York: Frederick A. Praeger, 1961); in Alexander Dallin, *Diversity in International Communism: A Documentary Record, 1961–63* (New York: Columbia University Press, 1963); and in William E. Griffith, *The Sino-Soviet Rift* (Cambridge, Mass.: M.I.T. Press, 1964).

9 "Problems of War and Strategy," *Selected Military Writings of Mao Tse-tung* (Peking: Foreign Languages Press, 1963), p. 272.

have been guided not by a desire to bring on a general war but by the perhaps correct calculation that more vigorous Soviet action would *not* lead to general nuclear war. Therefore, while the Chinese accept the legitimacy of the use of force, they also accept the need to avoid provoking the enemy and the tactical prudence of respecting him. Thus, their actual employment of force has been marked by their desire to pursue objectives as vigorously as possible short of provoking an American attack on the Chinese mainland. The Chinese Communists have always had to strike a balance between the two, and in doing so they appear to be acting so as to avoid provocation.

The Chinese Communists have resorted to the direct use of military force relatively rarely, and only when security objectives or the wish to reincorporate Chinese territory under the control of Peking seemed to be at issue. The Communist regime came to power by the direct use of military force. It ended the civil war at the boundaries of what had been Nationalist China, and, after its defeat at Quemoy in 1949, it suspended the attempt to capture Taiwan. But the Chinese Communists were to employ military force shortly thereafter in two major military ventures beyond their own borders. The first was the conquest of Tibet and its reincorporation into the Chinese state. The second, and apparently aggressive, action was their intervention in the Korean War. The Chinese were clearly not the moving force behind the decision in June, 1950, to have the North Korean army invade South Korea, for they were not ready to intervene to reunify Korea and bring it under Communist control. They showed signs of being willing to intervene only when the American forces crossed the 38th Parallel and appeared to be moving inexorably toward the Chinese Communist border. At this point, the Chinese made the difficult decision to commit their troops in the Korean War, apparently because they believed that failure to do so might jeopardize Communist control of the mainland. The Peking regime had not yet succeeded in quelling all the dissident groups in China and might well have felt that the establishment of American forces on the Chinese border would lead the United States to aid and support these counterrevolutionary groups. Hesitantly and with fear of an American atomic attack, the Chinese launched their armies on what was surprisingly, for them and for the rest of the world, a military victory over the advancing United Nations forces.[10] It is at least possible, if not likely, that a greater American willingness to employ threats, particularly the threat to use atomic weapons, might well have served to keep the Chinese out of the Korean War.[11]

The Chinese Communists have also from time to time employed military force in the Taiwan Straits, particularly in 1954–55 and again in 1958, but, given that the occupation of Taiwan remains a major objective of the Communist regime, its use of force in the Straits has not been as intensive as one might have expected. The Chinese Communists have been willing to move there only if they felt this would not mean a military encounter with the United States. Even in the two major crises in the Straits, their action has been limited to artillery fire and some light use of PT boats. They have refrained from bombing the islands or any ships heading for them.

Thus, for at least the first thirteen years of their control of the mainland, the Chinese resorted to military force only in areas which were traditionally part of China or, in the case of the Korean War, when they felt that their control over the mainland was in jeopardy. In 1962, however, in launching a military attack on the Sino-Indian border, the Chinese apparently departed from this policy. However, they did so only

[10] This interpretation of the Chinese entrance into the Korean War is based on Whiting, *China Crosses the Yalu.*
[11] For more extensive discussion of this point, see Morton H. Halperin, *Limited War in the Nuclear Age* (New York: John Wiley, 1963), pp. 50–53.

very briefly—when their surprisingly successful troops swept past the limits even of what the Chinese had claimed was the border. Again, this was in general a very limited use of military force—well below the level that might bring on American retaliation with nuclear weapons.[12]

Of much greater importance to the advancement of Chinese foreign-policy objectives in the Far East than the direct employment of military forces have been the more subtle threats that China *might* employ force, and the successful efforts to convince her neighbors that she is the dominant military power in the area with which they must come to terms. Combining implicit threats with the promise to respect the territorial integrity and political independence of their neighbors, the Chinese have managed to bring such countries as Cambodia and Burma within their general sphere of influence; most recently, they seem to be in the process of attempting the same with Pakistan. They have tried to convince these nations that China could move in to redress the boundaries to her own advantage or to aid indigenous Communist groups, but that she would not do so provided general Chinese foreign-policy control were accepted.

The exception is Indochina, where the Chinese Communist regime has had to deal from the outset with an active indigenous Communist movement that is capable of action on its own and that is clearly determined to seize power by force. But even in Indochina, the Chinese appear not to have done or to now be doing all that they can in terms of supplies and equipment and to have refrained completely from sending any "volunteers." Along the rest of their periphery, the Chinese prefer to rely on threats of military force rather than overt assistance to indigenous Communist groups. This is true

12 No satisfactory explanation has yet been provided of Chinese objectives in the Sino-Indian border dispute, and this is not the place to offer one. However, the basic Chinese willingness to use force to secure objectives, coupled with restraint, was demonstrated again, as was Peking's great tactical skill.

even in Burma, where such groups existed and where the presence of Chinese Nationalist forces might have enabled the Peking regime to justify intervention.[13]

Japan poses a very special case in Chinese foreign policy. The Peking regime recognized that Japan was the major prize in the competition between the United States and China for dominance in the Far East. At the same time, it recognized its inability to bring any direct military pressure to bear on Japan. Thus, Chinese policy toward Japan seems to combine general demonstrations of military strength (designed to convince members of the Japanese elite that they must eventually come to terms with Chinese power) with an appeal to the left-wing groups in Japan that are sympathetic to Communist China (designed to incite them to an eventual revolutionary overthrow of the conservative, pro-Western government.) After her nuclear detonation, China launched a propaganda attack against the new Japanese government and threatened Japan with nuclear devastation.[14]

In other parts of the world, far from their borders, the Chinese seem willing to be less cautious in supporting revolutionary groups and, in particular, in urging the Soviet Union to support revolutionary groups. Their own ability to intervene has been almost negligible, since they lack both airlift and sealift capability and the resources to give to guerrilla movements in Africa or Latin America. But they are willing, apparently, to do more than they have in the past, and are consolidating what is now possible by focusing their efforts in a few selected countries.

13 For a discussion of China's policy toward Burma that illustrates several of these points, see William C. Johnstone, *Burma's Foreign Policy: A Study in Neutralism* (Cambridge, Mass.: Harvard University Press, 1953), especially pp.158–200.

14 On Chinese policy contrasted with Soviet policy in Japan, see Paul F. Langer, "Moscow, Peking and Tokyo: Views and Approaches," in Kurt London (ed.), *Unity and Contradiction: Major Aspects of Sino-Soviet Relations* (New York: Frederick A. Praeger, 1962), pp. 207–32.

AMERICA VERSUS CHINA IN ASIA

The United States has been, and continues to be, concerned to prevent the domination of the Asian continent—and therefore of the Western Pacific—by a military power hostile to the United States. It was, ultimately, for this reason that the United States came into conflict with an expanding Japan; after the war, when the United States was still more actively involved in international affairs than she had been before, she very quickly conflicted with a powerful China seeking to extend her influence in Asia. This American-Chinese confrontation would have been likely had any strong regime come to power on the Chinese mainland. But the development of hostility was accelerated by the fact that the regime was a Communist one, coming to power at the time when the United States was just beginning to see the threat from Soviet Communism. Whatever was the precise nature of the Sino-Soviet relation through the 1950's, American officials viewed the Chinese regime as aligned to the Soviet Union, and hence looked upon Chinese expansion as part of the spread of a world-wide Communist system which it was necessary to oppose. For historical, geographical, and ideological reasons, the United States was hostile to the regime.[15]

The rise of a Communist regime on the Chinese mainland made more acute the problems for American foreign policy that would have existed in any case in the Far East. That is to say, the United States was thus faced with a direct challenge to the policy it had laid down in Asia as in the rest of the world (even in areas far from powerful Communist states)—to encourage the coming to power of durable, stable regimes

[15] This is not to imply that the United States would have been *equally* opposed to a strong, ambitious Nationalist government in China. Clearly it would not. But a clash between the United States and a powerful expansionist China would seem very likely in the long run regardless of China's form of government. The ideological elements have only brought the issue to a head more quickly.

capable of economic growth and, headed at least in the long run, for liberal democracy. The motives for this postwar American policy are complex ones, differing from individual to individual, from President to President, but the means have been clear: to this end, the United States has inaugurated vast economic aid programs, public information programs, and other programs of political and technical assistance.[16]

In addition to favoring internal, national stability, the United States has also favored the establishment of regional stability in the Far East—as well as in other areas of the world. It has been interested in preventing clashes between states of a common region, and in preventing the acceleration of arms races or in particular the acquisition of any kind of nuclear capability by local powers. Here again, American motives have been mixed. The United States reasons that regional instability, like domestic instability, makes the spread of Communism easier. But the American desire for peace in various areas of the world clearly embraces more than the pragmatics of "containment," for it is also dictated by factors other than the fear of the spread of Communism or even of the expansion of any local conflict into a major Soviet-American confrontation.[17]

Although political and economic policies are, perhaps, the critical ones in determining the success of American efforts in the Far East to stem Communist influence, it is obviously necessary in certain situations for the United States to employ or at least threaten to employ military force. In cases of overt Chinese aggression, it has been considered necessary to supply military equipment to the indigenous forces and in some cases

[16] This is not the place to argue whether these programs have in fact been effective in furthering American objectives. But, whatever else may be said of them, these programs demonstrate an *interest* on the part of the American Government in helping Asian countries to establish viable economic and democratic regimes.

[17] For analysis of the process by which the major powers are drawn into local conflict and the way in which they seek to limit them, see Halperin, *Limited War in the Nuclear Age*, pp. 1–38.

to send in American ground troops. The United States will also probably be forced to meet the relatively modest Chinese efforts to support revolutionary warfare by providing counter-insurgency assistance, as it has been doing in Vietnam and as it may be called on to do in other areas throughout the world. Moreover, the United States needs to create in the minds of Asian leaders the image that it is prepared to use force—to give military equipment and if necessary to commit American troops—to defend their countries against Chinese aggression.

In 1963, American policy with regard to the military threat from China was explored by the then Assistant Secretary of State for Far Eastern Affairs, Roger Hilsman, in a major speech on "United States Policy Toward Communist China":

> Our prime objective concerning Communist China is that it not subvert or commit aggression against its free world neigh-bors. It must not be allowed to accomplish for communism through force of arms that success which it has rarely achieved at the ballot box.
>
> President Kennedy called our purposes in the Far East "peaceful and defensive." And so they remain.
>
> If the free world governments of Asia are responsive to the needs and wishes of their own peoples, and if they have de-veloped the techniques and machinery for fulfilling the role of government in their countries, communism can endanger them only through the naked threat of military force. Most of the countries thus threatened are too small to stand alone against such a threat, and they need to use their resources for their people's welfare rather than for the creation of an elaborate war machine. We have undertaken in many cases to provide the protection against massive attack which will permit them to pursue their own destinies unafraid.
>
> Our military assistance in the Far East has been given with the objective of permitting Asian nations to develop the forces to defend their own borders and to protect themselves against probing attacks and paramilitary challenges. This is a necessary and grave responsibility.

However, I think that our hearts lie in that assistance which we can give in another direction: in helping them to establish the economic and political conditions in which a free society can flourish. This is particularly agreeable to us, because these are the things which those countries would want to do, and which we would want to help them to do, whether or not communism existed.[18]

THE PROSPECTS FOR *Détente*

In considering whether the hostility between the United States and China is likely to change or disappear, the first point to note is the one with which this chapter began—that the United States would oppose China's development of a nuclear capability even if China were not hostile to the United States. But there are other reasons to believe that the likelihood of a *rapprochement* between Communist China and the United States will be remote in the coming years. Even if there were no other disputes, the question of the continued Chinese Nationalist control of Taiwan would seem to make a major settlement impossible. The United States is politically too deeply committed to see Taiwan surrendered to the Chinese Communists, and the Peking regime is too committed to the liberation of Taiwan to accept any political settlement that excluded the cession of Taiwan to it. Eventually, this problem may be solved, but by then China will probably have acquired a substantial nuclear force.

If the problem of Taiwan did not exist, however, the real political conflict between the United States and China over the future orientation of South and Southeast Asia would still appear to make inevitable a clash between any powerful Chinese government and any determined American one. For there is genuine Sino-American conflict over the kinds of gov-

[18] Speech delivered before the Commonwealth Club, San Francisco, Calif., December 13, 1963. Text in U.S. Department of State *Bulletin*, L (January 6, 1964), 11–17.

ernment that Asian countries should have and what their basic orientation in international politics should be. The Chinese fear the establishment of a series of regimes allied to the United States, and the United States fears the spread of Chinese Communist influence. Even if one postulates that the ideological element of Chinese foreign policy will diminish, as it appears to be diminishing in the Soviet Union, it is again likely to be very many years away and preceded by the emergence of a Chinese nuclear force.

Nevertheless, some improvement in Sino-American relations is by no means impossible. Both governments have been willing to meet at international conferences dealing with Asian questions and in informal bilateral diplomatic talks. The opportunity exists for limited agreements when and if there is a sufficient overlapping of interests. Through Roger Hilsman's speech, the American Government suggested that it is ready for an improvement in relations:

> We do not know what changes may occur in the attitudes of future Chinese leaders. But if I may paraphrase a classic canon of our past, we pursue today towards Communist China a policy of the open door: we are determined to keep the door open to the possibility of change, and not to slam it shut against any developments which might advance our national good, serve the free world, and benefit the people of China. Patience is not unique to the Chinese. We too can maintain our positions without being provoked to unseemly action or despairing of what the future may hold. We will not sow the dragon's seed of hate which may bear bitter fruit in future generations of China's millions. But neither will we betray our interests and those of our allies to appease the ambitions of Communist China's leaders. We hope that, confronted with firmness which will make foreign adventure unprofitable, and yet offered the prospect that the way back into the community of man is not closed to it, the Chinese Communist regime will eventually forsake its present venomous hatreds which spring from a rigid class view of society. We hope that they will redis-

cover the Chinese virtue of tolerance for a multitude of beliefs and faiths; and that they will accept again a world of diversity, in place of the grey monolith which seems to be communism's goal for human society.[19]

But *rapprochement,* whatever its long-run prospects, and limited agreements, however valuable, still leave the United States with the necessity of dealing with a China armed with nuclear weapons. Before turning to a consideration of how American policy should deal with the threat that will be posed by a Chinese nuclear capability, it is necessary to explore the evolving Chinese attitude toward nuclear weapons and the likely dimensions of a Chinese nuclear capability in the coming years.

[19] *Ibid.,* p. 17.

2

Chinese Nuclear Strategy

Iɴ ᴛʜᴇ ᴘʀᴇᴄᴇᴅɪɴɢ ᴄʜᴀᴘᴛᴇʀ, ɪᴛ
was argued that in the past few years China has acted in international affairs in a relatively cautious and circumspect way,
and has been particularly concerned with avoiding a war with
the United States. Probably China would have sought to
avoid such armed confrontation even if the nuclear revolution had not occurred: America's conventional military
strength alone is an adequate deterrent to Chinese aggression.
Nevertheless, the fact that the United States possesses nuclear
weapons that it can use with less direct cost to itself than conventional arms would require has significantly affected Communist Chinese foreign policy since 1949. Before intervening
in Korea, the Chinese seem to have weighed the possibility of
the United States using nuclear weapons and the damage that
might result from an American attack.[1] Again, in its actions

[1] K. M. Panikkar, *In Two Chinas* (London: George Allen and Unwin, 1955),
p. 108.

24

in the Taiwan Straits, Peking was influenced by the desire to avoid a clash with the United States that might lead to the use of nuclear weapons. Thus it is possible at least to conjecture that China might have been more aggressive if the United States were not a nuclear power and that the Chinese have recognized the decisive importance of nuclear weapons in a Sino-American war.

It is more difficult to get a precise impression as to the kind of nuclear attack the Chinese considered likely. The Chinese have discussed the possibility both of an American strategic attack and of tactical use of atomic weapons by the United States. They appear to realize that use by the United States of a number of nuclear weapons could result not only in their military defeat but also in massive destruction of the Chinese mainland. Copies of the 1961 issues of the Chinese classified military publication *Work Correspondence* released by the United States Government in 1963 reveal that the Chinese then believed the United States would have to land troops in China even after a nuclear attack. At the same time, they admitted the great destructiveness of nuclear weapons alone. One American analyst has written:

> The documents suggest no Soviet assistance in case of war. The Chinese Communist do not appear to expect an immediate conflict with the United States but neither do they rule out the possibility of a surprise attack by American military forces. The fear of sudden moves by the United States presumably prompted a tightening of confidential and security work in 1961, for example. The *Work Correspondence* series highlights the Chinese Communist dread of nuclear and bacterial warfare on the one hand and the hope of attaining advanced weapons and technical expertise on the other. In several documents a shift in military training programs to prepare for scientific and technological advances in the coming few years is noted, but in the meantime the Chinese Communists have adopted a passive strategy of dispersal in order to survive nuclear attack and thence to wage "close combat" with invading group forces.

Maintenance of internal communications after nuclear attack has become a primary mission of radio and signal personnel.[2]

But the Chinese have also stressed the need to develop their own nuclear capability in order to deter nuclear threats from the United States. The Chinese Communists have undoubtedly overestimated the likelihood of the United States aiding Chiang Kai-shek's government to return to the Chinese mainland or seizing upon some excuse to attack China by herself. At least the Peking regime has not ruled out this possibility: According to one report, the Chinese Communists were training in 1948 for a possible large-scale battle in which "nuclear fortifications" would be attacked, which suggests that they feared American intervention with atomic weapons.[3]

It is much more difficult to estimate to what extent the Chinese feel their detonation of a nuclear device or their further development of a nuclear capability makes possible more aggressive action. They must still run the serious risk of American intervention with conventional armed forces, and they may recognize that American nuclear intervention will be more likely in certain situations, now that they have exploded an atomic device. It appears that the Chinese development of an atomic capability is related primarily to defensive objectives—to power status and subtle threats—rather than to specific plans to expand by the use of nuclear force.

2 John Wilson Lewis, *Chinese Communist Party Leadership and the Succession to Mao Tse-tung: An Appraisal of Tensions*, U.S. Department of State, Bureau of Intelligence and Research, Policy Research Study (Washington, January, 1964), p. 28. See also Ralph L. Powell, *Politico-Military Relationships in Communist China*, U.S. Department of State, Bureau of Intelligence and Research, Policy Research Study (Washington, October, 1963). Copies of the *Work Correspondence* are available from the Library of Congress in Chinese; an English translation is to be published by the Hoover Institution on War, Revolution, and Peace, Stanford University.

3 North Senshi News Agency, June 11, 1948. This quotation and all others from the period prior to 1957 are drawn (unless otherwise noted) from William Robert Harris, "The Adaptation of Communist Chinese Strategy to Nuclear and Thermonuclear Weapons (1945–1953)," a study now being prepared at the East Asian Research Center, Harvard University, under a U.S. Department of Defense contract on Studies of the Military in China.

Chinese Nuclear Doctrine[4]

The Nature of Nuclear War

It is widely held in the West that the Chinese Communists have an unrealistic view of nuclear warfare and that they do not recognize the great destruction it would cause—in China as in the rest of the world. Frequently, it is said that the Chinese believe that if even half their population were destroyed, they would still be able to dominate the world with the remainder of their millions of people. It is even argued that the Chinese actively desire a general nuclear war and in fact are likely to try to trigger an all-out nuclear exchange between the United States and the Soviet Union. A more moderate view, widely held among Western journalists, commentators, and, apparently, government officials, is that the Chinese, while not actively desiring a nuclear war, would not be unhappy if one were to take place and contemplate its outcome with relative equanimity.

The idea that the Chinese Communists lack knowledge of nuclear warfare and desire or are unafraid of nuclear war fits in with the popular image of the Peking regime as generally irrational and aggressive. (This view has been buttressed by the argument that the Chinese are in the early stage of their revolution, as compared to the Soviet Union, which is becoming more "bourgeois.") Until 1962, the Chinese themselves contributed to this argument with numerous statements

[4] In this section, I have sought to clarify current Chinese Communist nuclear doctrine, exploring—insofar as past developments are relevant to current attitudes—the evolution of this doctrine. My analysis of Chinese Communist doctrine prior to 1954 is based on research done by William Robert Harris, and of Chinese Communist doctrine from 1954 to 1960 on Alice Langley Hsieh, *Communist China's Strategy in the Nuclear Era* (Englewood Cliffs, N.J.: Prentice-Hall, 1962). Much information on current Chinese Communist doctrine has emerged from the Sino-Soviet polemics of the summer and fall of 1963, and in particular from the exchanges between the two governments over the nuclear test ban treaty. These documents are available in issues of the *Peking Review*, in pamphlets published by the Chinese and Soviet governments, and in Griffith, *The Sino-Soviet Rift*.

that appeared to underrate the effectiveness of nuclear weapons. For example, in October, 1960, a People's Liberation Army (PLA) official declared:

> The issue of a future war will not be decided by guided missiles or atom bombs. It will still be decided by man. Atom bombs will never be able to destroy mankind or the world. . . . The revolutionary people are always able to find ways and means for overcoming every kind of modern weapon.[5]

But the main impetus for this widespread belief in Chinese indifference to the results of nuclear war seems to come from the Soviet Union's deliberate effort to create such an impression among leaders of Communist parties and in the West generally. In a number of statements to Western visitors, Khrushchev alluded to Chinese irrationality concerning nuclear warfare, and the Russians repeatedly returned to this theme in their exchanges with the Chinese during 1963 and 1964. In a comment on the Chinese attitude toward the nuclear test ban, the Soviet Government stated:

> No Leninist-Communist could help experiencing a feeling of natural disgust at this attitude towards thermonuclear war: that there is nothing wrong even if half of humanity, if 300 million Chinese perish, for on the other hand imperialism would be erased from the face of the Earth and those who survive would rapidly create on the ruins of imperialism a new, a thousand times greater civilization. This very attitude to thermonuclear war has more than once been reflected in the pronouncements of high-ranking Chinese representatives. Even if the PRC Government makes not two but a hundred and two statements that it is longing for the prohibition and destruction of nuclear weapons, that its only concern is the interests of the peoples, it will not be able to wash away the shame of staking

[5] *People's Daily*, October 6–7, 1960. Cited by Alice Langley Hsieh, "Communist China and Nuclear Force," in R. N. Rosecrance (ed.), *The Dispersion of Nuclear Weapons: Strategy and Politics* (New York: Columbia University Press, 1964), p. 164.

the lives of hundreds of millions of people, including Chinese people, in a thermonuclear war.[6]

But the dispute between the Russians and the Chinese is really over the question how likely a thermonuclear war is, and not how destructive it would be. In fact, the public positions taken by Chinese and Soviet leaders on thermonuclear war are remarkably similar, despite the Russian assertions that they are different. They agree that general nuclear war can be avoided, and they agree that, should it nevertheless occur, imperialism would be doomed but Communism would survive. While they emphasize the destructiveness of nuclear war more, the Russians have not abandoned the notion that such a war would mean the end only of capitalism and not of Communism or of world civilization.

The question of whether to stress the destructiveness of nuclear war or the fact that Communism would nevertheless survive it is one with which Peking, as well as Moscow, has grappled since 1945 without any consistency of view. In what is the first known Chinese Communist statement on nuclear warfare (1945), Mao Tse-tung took the following line:

> Can atom bombs decide wars? No, they can't. Atom bombs could not make Japan surrender. Without the struggles waged by the people, atom bombs by themselves would be of no avail. If atom bombs could decide the war, then why was it necessary to ask the Soviet Union to send its troops? Why didn't Japan surrender when the atomic bombs were dropped on her and why did she surrender as soon as the Soviet Union sent troops? *Some of our comrades, too, believe that the atomic bomb is all-powerful;* that is a big mistake. . . . The theory that "weapons decide everything," the purely military viewpoint, a bureaucratic style of work divorced from the masses, individualist

[6] "Statement of the Soviet Government," August 21, 1963. Translation in *Moscow News,* reprinted in *Peking Review,* VI, No. 36 (September 6, 1963), 21–22. (Also available in Griffith, *The Sino-Soviet Rift,* Document 8; the text used there is the one that appeared in *Soviet News,* August 21, 1963.)

thinking, and the like—all these are bourgeois influences in our rank[s].[7] [Italics added.]

This downgrading of the importance of nuclear weapons (but not, as we shall see, of the possibility of avoiding nuclear war) was plausible so long as only a very small stockpile of fission weapons existed in both camps of the Cold War in the early years of the atomic age. By 1950, however, at the time of their entrance into the Korean War, the Chinese Communists had come to exaggerate, if anything, the destruction that nuclear weapons might cause, apparently estimating that if the United States were to attack China with atomic weapons as a result of her entry into the Korean War, they could suffer several millions of casualties.[8] Given the limited American stockpile and the likelihood that much of it would be saved for use against the Soviet Union in Europe if needed there, this was probably an overestimate. Nevertheless, the Chinese attempted to prepare their troops being sent into the Korean battle for such an event.[9]

At the same time, the Peking regime began to emphasize—in its propaganda and perhaps in its internal policy decisions—the strong possibility that the United States would be deterred from using nuclear weapons. The Chinese had become quite aware of the tremendous expansion of nuclear power both by the United States and by the Soviet Union, particularly their development of fusion weapons. Their original dread of the destruction that atomic weapons could cause now

[7] "The Situations and Our Policy After the Victory in the War of Resistance against Japan," dated August 13, 1945, in *Selected Works of Mao Tsetung*, IV, 21–22. There is reason to believe that this statement was not written until some time in the 1950's.

[8] See Panikkar, *In Two Chinas*, p. 108.

[9] See Herbert Goldhamer, "Communist Reaction in Korea to American Possession of the A-Bomb and Its Significance for U.S. Political and Psychological Warfare" (The RAND Corporation, RM-903, August 1, 1952), and "Chinese Concern about the A-Bomb" (The RAND Corporation, RM-987, November 7, 1952). Goldhamer's studies are based on interrogation of Chinese and North Korean prisoners of war.

fit the facts, and they lay greater stress than ever on the need and possibility of avoiding nuclear war.

If the behavior of the Chinese Communist regime during the early and mid-1950's suggests that the Chinese realized the possibility of the United States using nuclear weapons, that they feared this, and that they were determined to avoid provoking such use, it is also true that they were by no means ready to give up their initiative in foreign policy. (They continued now and again to disparage the usefulness of nuclear weapons; there was, apparently, a growing dispute within China on the extent to which nuclear weapons might be decisive in warfare.[10]) Indeed, addressing a closed session of the Moscow meeting of Communist and Workers' Parties on November 18, 1957, Mao Tse-tung argued for a more aggressive line to be taken by the entire international Communist movement:

At present another situation has to be taken into account, *namely, that the war maniacs may drop atomic and hydrogen bombs everywhere.* They drop them and we act after their fashion; thus there will be chaos and lives will be lost. The question has to be considered for the worst. The Political Bureau of our Party has held several sessions to discuss this question. If fighting breaks out now, China has got only hand-grenades and not atomic bombs—which the Soviet Union has though. Let us imagine, how many people will die if war should break out? Out of the world's population of 2,700 million, one third—or, if more, half—may be lost. *It is they and not we who want to fight;* when a fight starts, atomic and hydrogen bombs may be dropped. I debated this question with a foreign statesman. He believed that if an atomic war was fought, the whole of mankind would be annihilated. I said that if the worst came to the worst and half of mankind died, the other half would remain while imperialism would be razed to the ground and

10 See Hsieh, *Communist China's Strategy in the Nuclear Age,* pp. 15–75, and Harris, "The Adaptation of Communist Chinese Strategy to Nuclear and Thermonuclear Weapons," for contrasting views on the nature of the debate.

the whole world would become socialist; in a number of years there would be 2,700 million people again and definitely more. *We Chinese have not yet completed our construction and we desire peace.* However, *if imperialism insists on fighting a war, we will have no alternative but to make up our minds and fight to the finish before going ahead with our construction.* If every day you are afraid of war and war eventually comes, what will you do then? First I have said that the East wind prevails over the West wind and that war will not break out, and now I have added these explanations about the situation in case war should break out. In this way both possibilities have been taken into account.[11]

When the Chinese released the text of this speech in the autumn of 1963, during the debate over a nuclear test ban, the Russians alleged that it was a "corrected" version of Mao's statement, which, while accurately quoting most of Mao's remarks, changed the emphasis in order to suggest that the Chinese desire to avoid nuclear war was greater than it actually was. They claimed, for example, that Mao's statement in relation to "the construction of socialism" in China actually read as follows: "In China construction has not got under way in earnest. If the imperialists impose a war on us, we shall be prepared to terminate the construction; let us first have a trial of strength, and then return to construction."[12]

But the Chinese were adamant: Perhaps their most optimistic statement on the outcome of a nuclear war—which had appeared in *Red Flag* on November 8, 1960, in an article

11 The text of this speech was released by the Chinese Government on September 1, 1963, in "Statement by the Spokesman of the Chinese Government —A Comment on the Soviet Government's Statement of August 21." Translation in *Peking Review*, VI, No. 36 (September 6, 1963), 10. (Also in Griffith, *op. cit.*, Document 9, p. 376.)

12 "A Reply to Peking—Soviet Government Statement," published in Moscow newspapers on September 21 and 22, 1963. Translation published as *Soviet Booklet No. 122* (London: Soviet Booklets, 1963), pp. 20–21. (Also, reprinted from *Soviet News*, September 23–24, 1963, in Griffith, *op. cit.*, Document 12.) It seems unlikely that eight years after the establishment of a Communist regime in China, Mao would say that construction had not yet gotten under way.

entitled "Long Live Leninism!"—was now cited again to the Russians:

> *We consistently oppose the launching of criminal wars by imperialism,* because imperialist war would impose enormous sacrifices upon the people of various countries (including the peoples of the United States and other imperialist countries). But *should the imperialists impose such sacrifices on them,* we believe that, just as the experience of the Russian revolution and the Chinese revolution shows, those sacrifices would not be in vain. The victorious people would very swiftly create on the ruins of imperialism a civilization thousands of times higher than the capitalist system and a truly beautiful future for themselves.[13] [Italics added.]

The Chinese Communists went on to insist: "The meaning of these words is very clear: (1) China wants peace, and not war; (2) it is the imperialists, and not we, who want to fight; (3) a world war can be prevented; and (4) even in the eventuality that imperialism should impose a war on the people of the world and inflict tragic losses on them, it is the imperialist system, and not mankind, that would perish, and the future of mankind would still be bright.[14]

Indeed, the Chinese asserted that the Soviet Union shared their view that socialism would survive a nuclear war:

> While propagating the theory of the annihilation of mankind, they say that the people of the world will bury imperialism if imperialism forces a nuclear war on them. For instance, the Open Letter of the Central Committee of the C.P.S.U. of July 14 declared, "It stands to reason, of course, that if the imperialist madmen unleash a war, the peoples will sweep away capitalism and bury it." But people are bound to ask, if according to

[13] Quoted in "Statement by the Spokesman of the Chinese Government— A Comment on the Soviet Government's Statement of August 21." The complete text of "Long Live Leninism!" is reprinted in Hudson, *The Sino-Soviet Dispute,* pp. 82–112.

[14] "Statement by the Spokesman of the Chinese Government—A Comment on the Soviet Government's Statement of August 21."

your theory all the 3,000 million people in the world will die if imperialism unleashes a nuclear war, then who would remain to bury imperialism?[15]

The Chinese rendition of the "Open Letter" is accurate. But the Soviet statement had gone on to say: "The Communists, representing the peoples, the true advocates of socialist humanism, are called upon to do everything they can to prevent another world war in which hundreds of millions of people would perish."[16]

It seems clear that the Chinese are not now trying to capitalize on the fact that in the West they are considered irrationally unafraid of nuclear warfare. In fact, the Chinese have gone out of their way—not only in the items quoted, but in radio programs broadcast throughout the world and in their propaganda journal the *Peking Review*—to stress that they are not "bad" men who "welcome" a nuclear war. There is little doubt that they recognize the destruction that would come to China in a nuclear war and that their policy is geared to prevent such a war. At a press conference in Somalia during his African trip in 1964, Chou En-lai, when asked whether it were true that "in the event of a nuclear war China feels she is less vulnerable than any other country on the globe and that she would hope to emerge victorious from such a war which might destroy the rest of the world," replied that "this is fabrication, pure and simple. . . . If a nuclear war breaks out, China would lose more people than would other countries. . . . It is with ulterior motives that the imperialists and certain other persons unscrupulously have distorted China's position and made widespread propaganda about it."[17]

15 *Loc. cit.*

16 "The Open Letter of the Central Committee of the Communist Party of the Soviet Union to Party Organizations and all Communists of the Soviet Union," *Pravda*, July 14, 1963. Translation in *Current Soviet Documents*, I (August 5, 1963), 18. (Also, reprinted from *Soviet News*, July 17, 1963, in Griffith, *op. cit.*, Document 3.)

17 Interview with Agence France Press, February 3, 1964. Text in *Peking Review*, VII, No. 7 (February 14, 1964), 16.

The difference between the Chinese stress on Communism surviving a nuclear war and the Russian emphasis on the destruction in nuclear war probably stems from the fact that the Chinese, being themselves still without a nuclear deterrent force, are reluctant to emphasize deterrence and mutual destruction. They have, indeed, been quite candid in discussing this dilemma; in late 1962, it was put as follows:

We hold that in order to mobilize the masses of the people against nuclear war and nuclear weapons it is necessary to inform them of the enormous destructiveness of these weapons. It would be patently wrong to underestimate this destructiveness. However, U.S. imperialism is doing its utmost to disseminate dread of nuclear weapons in pursuit of its policy of nuclear blackmail. In these circumstances, while Communists should point out the destructiveness of nuclear weapons, they should counter the U.S. imperialist propaganda of nuclear terror by stressing the possibility of outlawing them and preventing nuclear war; they should try and transmute the people's desire for peace into righteous indignation at the imperialist policy of nuclear threats and lead the people to struggle against the U.S. imperialist policies of aggression and war. In no circumstances must Communists act as voluntary propagandists for the U.S. imperialist policy of nuclear blackmail. We hold that the U.S. imperialist policy of nuclear blackmail must be thoroughly exposed and that all peace-loving countries and people must be mobilized on the most extensive scale to wage an unrelenting fight against every move made by the U.S. imperialists in their plans for aggression and war. We are deeply convinced that, by relying on the united struggle of all forces defending peace, it is possible to frustrate the U.S. imperialist policy of nuclear blackmail. This is the correct and effective policy for achieving a ban on nuclear weapons and preventing a nuclear war.[18]

[18] The Differences between Comrade Togliatti and Us," *People's Daily,* December 31, 1962. Translation in *Peking Review,* VI, No. 1 (January 4, 1963), 12–13.

The Likelihood of Nuclear War

There has been perhaps as much misunderstanding of the Chinese view on the likelihood of nuclear warfare as of their interpretation of its nature and consequences. The Chinese have never claimed that nuclear war is inevitable, but they have denied that peace can be attained through conciliation and disarmament rather than through building up military strength and militantly opposing imperialism. Secondly, they have differed with the Russians over the possibility and desirability of avoiding local wars, and over the relation between local wars and the likelihood of a general war.

Mao Tse-tung's earliest statement on the possibility of avoiding world war was made in a speech of December 25, 1947, in which he declared: "If everyone makes strenuous efforts, we, together with all the democratic forces of the world, can surely defeat the imperious plan of enslavement, prevent the outbreak of a third world war, overthrow all reactionary regimes, and win lasting peace for mankind."[19] Since then, the Chinese have made no efforts to conceal their belief that war could be avoided. They explicitly accepted the Khrushchevian reinterpretation of Leninism which holds that the Socialist camp is now strong enough to prevent imperialism from launching a world war. Not long ago, in fact, the Western press was taken to task for failing to recognize that China as well as Russia accepted this modification:

> It doesn't take the "free" Western press long to catch on! After years of harping on the theme of China's supposed "warlike intent" and theory of the "inevitability of war"—a game of make-believe in which the Soviet press has more recently joined —both the London and New York *Times* on October 2 made a brilliant discovery of the obvious.
>
> Taking up a Reuters dispatch from Peking the two eminent

[19] "The Present Situation and Our Tasks," dated December 25, 1947, in *Selected Works of Mao Tse-tung*, IV, 173.

Times displayed shock headlines: "China Hints at New Attitude to War" and "Red China Eases Stand on Inevitability of War." They found their "new attitude" in the National Day speech of Peking's Mayor Peng Chen, who said that with world unity, "a new world war can be prevented, world peace can be preserved and the future of mankind is infinitely bright." This, they said, quoting Reuters' man in Peking, was seen by "observers" as "a new formulation of the Chinese attitude to the future of the world."

All we can say is that, like the "observers" in Peking, the *Times*' China experts have neglected their homework rather badly. Where have they been for the last three years—and longer? What Peng Chen said on National Day should not be news to anyone remotely concerned with China. For years China's leaders and newspapers have been saying that "world war can be prevented if the peoples of the world unite."[20]

The article went on to quote statements by various Chinese Communist leaders in 1960, 1961, and 1962 to demonstrate that China did not publicly take the line that world war is inevitable after 1960. The Chinese leaders reiterated this view in the statement released when the Chinese nuclear bomb was detonated on October 16, 1964, that "we hope a nuclear war would never occur."[21] What, then, has been the difference between the Russian and Chinese views on the inevitability of war?

While accepting the proposition that a nuclear exchange between the United States and the Sino-Soviet bloc can be avoided, the Chinese have argued that neither local wars nor wars of national liberation can be avoided. They define local wars, as Khrushchev did in his widely quoted speech of January 6, 1961, as wars started by the United States; wars of national liberation are wars started by indigenous Communist

20 *Peking Review*, VI, No. 44 (November 1, 1963), 19–20.
21 "Official Statement of the Chinese People's Republic," released by New China News Agency (NCNA), October 16, 1964; text in *The New York Times*, October 17, 1964, p. 10. Hereinafter referred to as the Chinese "Detonation Statement."

or nationalist forces.[22] Khrushchev—there and elsewhere—spoke of the need to provide opposing forces in local wars and to support wars of national liberation, but in general the Russians tend to warn that there is a high probability of local wars exploding into general nuclear war and that they must therefore be avoided. The Chinese, on the other hand, argue that both are virtually inevitable:

> It is one thing to prevent a world war and another to eliminate all wars. Imperialism and the reactionaries are the source of war. In conditions where imperialism and reactionaries still exist, it is possible that wars of one kind or another may occur. The history of the seventeen postwar years shows that local wars of one kind or another have never ceased. Oppressed nations and oppressed people are bound to rise in revolution. When imperialism and the reactionaries employ armed forces to suppress revolution, it is inevitable that civil wars and national-liberation wars will occur. Marxist-Leninists have always maintained that only after the imperialist system has been overthrown and only after all systems of oppression of man by man and of exploitation of man by man have been abolished, and not before, will it be possible to eliminate all wars and to reach "a world without war."[23]

Thus the Chinese seriously disagree with the Russians on two points concerning wars below the level of nuclear world war. The Chinese argue that the Sino-Soviet bloc must be prepared to aid groups fighting wars of national liberation against imperialist and neo-imperialist regimes. They also argue that, when the West intervenes in such conflicts, it is necessary for the Sino-Soviet bloc to counter this intervention with intervention of their own. The Chinese argue these points specifically in relation to the Algerian revolution and events in the Middle East in 1958. The Chinese accuse the

22 The Khrushchev speech has been widely reprinted, as, for example, in Hudson, *op. cit.*, pp. 207–21.
23 "The Differences between Comrade Togliatti and Us," p. 15.

Soviet leaders of being cowards who believe that a single spark can ignite a nuclear war and that it is therefore necessary to avoid intervention in any local war and to seek revolution by peaceful means. The Chinese deny that nuclear weapons have changed these basic obligations of socialist regimes:

> The leaders of the CPSU hold that with the appearance of nuclear weapons there is no longer any difference between just and unjust wars. . . . They hold that with the appearance of nuclear weapons the oppressed peoples and nations must abandon revolution and refrain from waging just popular revolutionary wars and wars of national liberation. . . . In short, according to the leaders of the CPSU, with the emergence of nuclear weapons, the contradiction between the socialist and the imperialist camps, the contradiction between the proletariat and the bourgeoisie in the capitalist countries, and the contradiction between the oppressed nations and imperialism have all disappeared. . . . They regard the contradictions in the contemporary world as boiling down to a single contradiction, that is, their fictitious contradiction between the so-called common survival of imperialism and the oppressed classes and nations on the one hand and their total destruction on the other.[24]

Wars of national liberation must be supported, the Chinese argue, because they are the only way in which Communist regimes can be installed. The Chinese point out that Communist regimes have never been established by a peaceful takeover of power, that to abandon violence is to abandon the spread of revolution. The Chinese also argue that the Russians greatly overestimate the danger of a national-liberation war or Soviet intervention in a local war leading to general nuclear war for, they say, the pressures militating against all-

[24] "Two Different Lines on the Question of War and Peace—Comment on the Open Letter of the Central Committee of the CPSU [V]," dated November 19, 1963. Translation in *Peking Review*, VI, No. 47 (November 22, 1963), 11–12. (Also in Griffith, *op. cit.*, Document 16, p. 485.)

out war are very great. Resolute and united action by the Socialist camp can prevent nuclear war, they contend, but not efforts to appease the imperialist powers or stress on peaceful co-existence and disarmament.[25] The Chinese claim that history in the postwar period has borne them out:

> In recent years, certain persons have been spreading the argument that a single spark from a war of national liberation or from a revolutionary people's war will lead to a world conflagration destroying the whole of mankind. What are the facts? Contrary to what these persons say, the wars of national liberation and the revolutionary people's wars that have occurred since World War II have not led to world war. The victory of these revolutionary wars has directly weakened the forces of imperialism and greatly strengthened the forces which prevent the imperialists from launching a world war and which defend world peace. Do not the facts demonstrate the absurdity of this argument?[26]

Local wars and wars of national liberation, the Chinese argue, then, are not only inevitable but desirable and necessary to expand the area of Communism. History demonstrates, they continue, that "popular" wars, instead of being dangerous, as the Russians have suggested, do not lead to general nuclear war. On the contrary, the failure of the Sino-Soviet bloc to take an aggressive stance only encourages the Western powers and makes such war more likely: General nuclear war can and must be prevented by the unity and action of the socialist camp. It is only an absurd fear of escalation into general nuclear war that keeps the Soviet Union from rendering the proper assistance to national liberation movements.

[25] By putting "united" in their formula, the Chinese leave themselves free to criticize the Soviet Union for "adventurism" (as they did in the Cuba crisis) and to advocate their possession of nuclear weapons.

[26] "A Proposal Concerning the General Line of the International Communist Movement: The Letter of the Central Committee of the Communist Party of China in Reply to the Letter of the Central Committee of the Communist Party of the Soviet Union of March 30, 1963," dated June 14, 1963. Translation in *Peking Review*, VI, No. 25 (June 21, 1963), 14. (Also in Griffith, *op. cit.*, Document 2, p. 274.)

The Role of the Strategic Balance

Far from deprecating the influence of nuclear weapons on the course of international politics, the Chinese have tended to overestimate the importance of a strategic nuclear balance. In the early years of the atomic era, the Chinese were apparently very conscious of the danger posed for them by the United States' atomic monopoly, and they greeted the announcement of Russia's first nuclear test with obvious relief: "The Soviet Union has recently declared that she had atomic weapons for some time already. This declaration is a heavy blow to the instigators of atomic war. Thus it is clear that we will certainly have sufficient strength to pulverize all the criminal plots of the warmongers."[27] Then again, during 1951 and 1952, the Chinese became increasingly nervous over signs of the American development of a thermonuclear capability. It was with great relief that the Chinese announced (they were the first openly to do so) the Soviet H-bomb test in August, 1953, breaking their two-year silence on hydrogen weapons. Even then, their recognition of the continued American superiority in nuclear weapons from 1955 on led to growing public discussion and, so far as we know, official concern about the ever-increasing American stockpile of strategic nuclear weapons.

The period of China's greatest fear of the nuclear imbalance ended suddenly in 1957 with the launching of the Soviet Sputnik and with the Soviet Union's ICBM test. The Chinese concluded that a fundamental change had taken place in the psychological balance of power and would soon do so in the military balance: The East wind was now prevailing over the West wind. Addressing the Moscow Conference on November 18, 1957, Mao declared:

27 Radio Peking, International Service in English Morse to North America, October 4, 1949.

It is my opinion that the international situation has now
reached a new turning point. There are two winds in the world
today, the East wind and the West wind. There is a Chinese
saying, "Either the East wind prevails over the West wind or
the West wind prevails over the East wind." *It is characteristic
of the situation today,* I believe, *that the East wind is prevailing over the West wind. That is to say, the forces of socialism
are overwhelmingly superior to the forces of imperialism.*[28]

Beginning in 1957, the Chinese urged the Soviet Union to
take advantage of the changing strategic balance and to press
for the victory of socialism.

By 1960, however, the Chinese began to have second
thoughts about the effect of the 1957 change in the strategic
balance. It was not that they doubted that the fundamental
change had occurred; rather, they came to recognize that the
Soviet Union was not inclined to share their radical estimate
of it, and were not prepared—or so it seemed to the Chinese—
to press the political advantages that stemmed from the new
military situation. On the contrary, the Chinese thought the
Russians were moving toward a *détente* with the West—using
their new military strength, as it were, to effect a political
settlement that would leave China's demands for Taiwan and
her recognition as a major world power unfulfilled. At the
same time, the Chinese were alarmed by evidence that the
United States was increasing the size of her defense budget
and might soon redress the strategic balance that the Chinese
believed (incorrectly) was then in the Soviet Union's favor.[29]

It seems clear first that the Chinese overestimated the 1957
change in the strategic balance of power and secondly that

[28] Cited in "Statement by the Spokesman of the Chinese Government—A
Comment on the Soviet Government's Statement of August 21."

[29] This interpretation of the Chinese attitude in 1960, and the more general
assertion on the significance the Chinese attach to the over-all strategic balance, are based on A. M. Halpern, "Communist China and Peaceful Co-Existence," *China Quarterly*, No. 3 (July–September, 1960), pp. 16–31. The original
RAND version of this paper bore the more descriptive title "Why Are the
Chinese Nervous?", The RAND Corporation, P-1987, July 5, 1960.

they never were informed in great detail by the Soviet Union as to its nature. The Soviet Union has, in fact, accused the Chinese of speaking out of ignorance:

> Of course we cannot now divulge such things as, for instance, the concrete results of the nuclear weapon tests we carried out in 1961–62, information on the calibres of the nuclear warheads in our arsenal, the purpose of specific nuclear combat devices of which the Soviet Union has an abundance, where these combat devices are deployed, and so forth. That would be against the security interests of the Soviet Union and of all the socialist states, including the security interests of the People's Republic of China.
>
> And if the Chinese leaders, in saying that in recent years the situation has not changed but the U.S.S.R. policy on a test ban has, thus try in a way to provoke the Soviet Union to demonstrate clearly the changes in the balance of nuclear strength in recent years and for this purpose to divulge the defence secrets of U.S.S.R., we can tell them one thing only: while you are talking about your concern to strengthen the defence of the socialist countries, you are in actual fact playing the role of those who do not cherish the security interests of the socialist community but are ready to play into the hands of the forces of imperialist reaction. The Chinese leaders cannot be unaware of the fact that obtaining really reliable information on Soviet nuclear and missile weapons is exactly what the military staffs of certain powers and aggressive military blocs dream of.[30]

By 1963, then, in attempting to justify the decision to sign the nuclear test ban treaty, the Soviet Union argued that the balance of military force had changed from the earlier time, when they had felt that a three-environment test ban treaty would not be in their interests, and now made peaceful coexistence and economic and political competition for the underdeveloped areas possible. The Chinese, on the other hand, were now in the position of having to suggest that there had been virtually no change in the balance between 1961–62

[30] "Statement of the Soviet Government," August 21, 1963.

and 1963. In 1964, to justify their nuclear test, they stressed that their development of nuclear weapons would have an important effect on the nuclear balance of power.

THE NEED FOR A CHINESE NUCLEAR CAPABILITY

China's commitment of resources to the development of a nuclear capability makes it clear that she assigns a high priority to the goal of becoming a militarily effective nuclear power—a goal determined by the fundamental aspiration to make China a great power. More specifically, this high-priority goal may be explained in terms of the following: (1) the desire for a more credible deterrent against an American attack; (2) the desire for increased influence within the Communist world; (3) the desire for additional means of supporting wars of national liberation; and (4) the desire for additional means for establishing Chinese hegemony in Asia.

Deterring an American Attack

The statement issued by the New China News Agency announcing the detonation of a nuclear bomb on October 16, 1964, explained the significance of the event in this way:

> This is a major achievement of the Chinese people in their struggle to increase their national defense capability and oppose the United States imperialist policy of nuclear blackmail and nuclear threats.
>
> To defend oneself is the inalienable right of every sovereign state. And to safeguard world peace is the common task of all peace-loving countries.
>
> China cannot remain idle and do nothing in the face of the ever-increasing nuclear threat posed by the United States. China is forced to conduct nuclear tests and develop nuclear weapons. . . . The development of nuclear weapons by China is for defense and for protecting the Chinese people from the danger of the United States' launching a nuclear war.

The Chinese have argued consistently that the more Socialist countries that have nuclear weapons, the more successful
deterrence is likely to be—an argument analogous to one advanced by certain groups in Great Britain and France.[31] This
theme was expressed in a *People's Daily* editorial on August
9, 1962, for instance. The editorial noted that China has
consistently opposed nuclear tests and favored the banning of
nuclear weapons, but it continued:

> We hold, however, that when imperialism is stubbornly hinder-
> ing and opposing agreement on the suspension of nuclear tests
> and the prohibition of nuclear weapons and is using such
> weapons to threaten the people of the world, the Socialist
> countries, to ensure the security of the Socialist camp and
> defend world peace, naturally must possess nuclear weapons,
> and moreover, nuclear weapons of better quality than those of
> U.S. imperialism.
>
> The Socialist countries love peace; nuclear weapons in their
> hands and nuclear tests conducted by them are entirely differ-
> ent in nature from nuclear weapons in the hands of the im-
> perialist bloc and nuclear tests conducted by that bloc. The
> possession of nuclear weapons and the carrying out of nuclear
> tests by the Socialist countries can only be a telling blow against
> the imperialist policy of the nuclear arms drive and nuclear
> blackmail and therefore helps to prevent war; it will help
> force imperialism to accept some kind of agreement on the dis-
> continuance of nuclear testing and the prohibition of nuclear
> weapons and so will help the cause of world peace.[32]

A January 5, 1963, *Red Flag* editorial underlined the Chinese determination to be in a position to resist nuclear blackmail and to build up the strength of the socialist countries.
Two themes that were to accompany this argument in later
statements were introduced: The first was that the People's

[31] The Chinese have sometimes argued that *any* increase in the number of
countries possessing nuclear weapons is desirable. See, for example, Chen Yi's
interview with the Reuters manager Walton Cole, October 5, 1961.

[32] Abridged translation in *Peking Review*, V, No. 33 (August 17, 1962), 10.

Republic of China sought in the first instance an agreement on atomic-free zones in the Pacific region "embracing all the countries there, including the U.S.A.," and in the long run general and complete disarmament; the second was that the socialist camp would never and should never use nuclear weapons to engage in nuclear gambles—an obvious reference to the Cuban missile crisis of October, 1962.[33]

With the opening of the nuclear test ban talks, the Chinese maintained that they would not be a party to a test ban agreement unless it stipulated the total prohibition of the possession of nuclear weapons by all countries. In an apparent effort to prevent the Soviet Union from signing any test ban treaty at all, China warned that "the United States can use suspension to create a pressure of public opinion to prevent socialist countries other than the Soviet Union from conducting nuclear tests and possessing nuclear capability, thus preventing the socialist camp from reinforcing its power to resist U.S. nuclear blackmail."[34]

The Russians replied that, in effect, Soviet nuclear power was great enough to protect the socialist camp and that a test ban treaty was a sign of strength rather than weakness, but the Chinese refused to back down. While acknowledging the danger of the spread of nuclear weapons to more countries, particularly to Germany, they discussed in detail the need for a number of national nuclear forces in the socialist camp:

> In fighting imperialist aggression and defending its security, every socialist country has to rely in the first place on its own defence capability, and then—and only then—on assistance from fraternal countries and the people of the world. For the Soviet statement to describe all the socialist countries as depending on the nuclear weapons of the Soviet Union for their survival

---

[33] Printed in the British Broadcasting Corporation's Summary of World Broadcasts (hereafter cited as BBC SWB), FE/1142/C/1.

[34] "U.S. Nuclear Fraud Exposed," *People's Daily*, July 19, 1963. Translation in *Peking Review*, VI, No. 30 (July 26, 1963), 47.

is to strike an out-and-out great-power chauvinistic note and to fly in the face of the facts.

The Chinese Government has always fully appreciated the importance of the Soviet Union's possession of nuclear weapons. However, such possession must in no way be made a justification for preventing other socialist countries from increasing their own defence capabilities. . . . If the Soviet Government is earnest about abiding by the Moscow Statement and really wants to fight the imperialist policies of aggression and war and to defend world peace, there is no reason why it should try so hard to obstruct other socialist countries from increasing their defence capabilities.

With regard to preventing nuclear proliferation, the Chinese Government has always maintained that the arguments of the U.S. imperialists must not be echoed, but that a class analysis must be made. Whether or not nuclear weapons help peace depends on who possesses them. It is detrimental to peace if they are in the hands of imperialist countries; it helps peace if they are in the hands of socialist countries. It must not be said undiscriminatingly that the danger of nuclear war increases along with the increase in the number of nuclear powers. Nuclear weapons were first the monopoly of the United States. Later, the Soviet Union also came to possess them. Did the danger of nuclear war become greater or less when the number of nuclear powers increased from one to two? We say it became less, not greater.

Nuclear weapons in the possession of a socialist country are always a means of defence against nuclear blackmail and nuclear war. So long as the imperialists refuse to ban nuclear weapons, the greater the number of socialist countries possessing them, the better the guarantee of world peace. A fierce class struggle is now going on in the world. In this struggle, the greater the strength on our side, the better. Does it make sense to say the less the better?[35]

35 "Statement by the Spokesman of the Chinese Government—A Comment on the Soviet Government's Statement of August 3," dated August 15, 1963. Translation in *Peking Review*, VI, No. 33 (August 15, 1963), pp. 12–13. (Also in Griffith, *op. cit.*, Document 7, p. 340.)

The Chinese position as it is presented here—that the more socialist countries with nuclear weapons the better, because multiple forces increase the general strength of the socialist camp and because they increase deterrence by making more credible in the eyes of the United States the likelihood of a nuclear response—would seem to suggest the argument that nuclear weapons are necessary for China not in case of any breakdown in the Sino-Soviet alliance but merely because they add to the over-all strength and credibility of the Communist bloc's deterrence. However, the Chinese went beyond this to argue that the Soviet Union has tried to use her nuclear dominance to control the socialist camp and that she has not put nuclear weapons at the disposal of other socialist countries or cast a protective umbrella over wars of national liberations when she should have. In addition, the Chinese suggest that since the aim of the test ban agreement was apparently *détente* with the West, the Soviet Union may in the future be even less willing to use her nuclear strength to promote the aims of other socialist countries and perhaps to protect them against American nuclear threats. At present, however, the Chinese assert that Russia will in fact come to China's aid in the event of an American attack. Thus, Chou En-lai told newsmen in Cairo in 1963, that "in the event of emergency, the Chinese and Soviet peoples will without fail stand by each other, shoulder-to-shoulder, hand-in-hand."[36] In the absence of Soviet support, the Chinese would probably try to deter the United States by making retaliatory threats directed at Asian countries. In order to accomplish this, it appears, they are seeking to develop an intermediate-range missile force that could be targeted on Asian cities. The Chinese could expect such a force to serve as a powerful deterrent against an American attack on China resulting from the expansion of a Sino-American conflict on her borders.

[36] *Peking Review*, VI, No. 52 (December 27, 1963), 14.

Influence Within the Communist Bloc

In their "Detonation Statement," the Chinese Communist leaders made only passing reference to their dispute with the Soviet Union or to the need for China to develop a nuclear capability in order to combat Soviet influence in the international Communist movement. They remarked simply that the test ban treaty "tried to consolidate the nuclear monopoly held by the three nuclear powers and tie up the hands and feet of all peace-loving countries."

Long before the Chinese were prepared to discuss openly conflicts within the Communist bloc over nuclear strategy, however, they had debated this issue in the guise of considering the contradictions arising within NATO over nuclear strategy. For example, in February, 1963, in an article on "Imperialist Contradictions Around the Question of Great Nuclear-Power Status," a Chinese commentator declared: "A country which has fine delivery vehicles (long-range missiles and guided missiles) and a large quantity of nuclear bombs of great variety is a super state, and only a super state is qualified to lead the world and to control and direct those countries which do not have nuclear weapons or have only a small number of nuclear weapons without fine delivery vehicles."[37] The article went on to describe how the United States desired to control Europe, the United Kingdom desired to control France, and France desired to control West Germany. It concluded:

Today, the United States is attempting to assert its leadership and impose the second-class nation status on the imperialist countries of Western Europe. That is why this sharp contradiction has developed to such an unprecedented degree. . . . All

[37] Ouyang Hsing, "Imperialist Contradictions Around the Question of Great Nuclear-Power Status," *China Youth*, Nos. 3–4, February 10, 1963. Translation in *Selections from China Mainland Magazine*, No. 355 (Hong Kong: American Consulate General, 1963), p. 18.

these are indications that France will not give up its own independent nuclear force and deprive itself of the great nuclear-power status, to the point of handing over the military security and political future of its own and those of the Common Market as a whole to U.S. control.[38]

Through the early months of 1963, the Chinese newspapers, radio, and New China News Agency released a series of articles highlighting the growing stresses and strains in the NATO alliance over the question of national nuclear forces. The broadcasts expressed sympathy for the French position and described the multilateral force as a crude attempt by the United States to continue her control over the NATO countries by being the only power to control nuclear weapons. While the Chinese never openly drew the relevant analogies to their own situation, prior to the intensification of the Sino-Soviet controversy at the time of the test ban negotiations in June, the implication of their remarks was clear.[39]

Allusions to the situation in Europe, and in particular to French opposition to American nuclear policy, continued after the signing of the nuclear test ban treaty. For example, NCNA reported on July 24, 1963, that French newspapers and news agencies had all expressed strong opposition to the Americans' intention to bar France from developing an independent nuclear force and to weaken her resistance to their efforts to control the allies through nuclear superiority. According to NCNA, the French papers maintained that the United States tried to use the possibility of a test ban agreement to attain its aims but that France had clearly indicated

[38] *Ibid.*, pp. 18, 21.

[39] Among the many programs and dispatches that could be cited, see, for example: Peking Home Service broadcast, January 8, 1963, at 12:10 GMT (in BBC SWB, FE/1145/A1/2, January 10, 1963); NCNA dispatch from London, January 10, 1963 (in BBC SWB, FE/1147/A1/1, January 12, 1963); and a Peking Home Service broadcast, February 21, 1963, at 12:10 GMT (in BBC SWB, FE/1183/A1/2, February 23, 1963). See also Yang Chun-fong, "A Nuclear Force Without a Name," *Peking Review*, VI, No. 24 (June 14, 1963), 9–13.

it would never be bound by such an agreement.[40] Thus the Chinese have sought to make their case for a Chinese nuclear capability by analogy, by stressing France's need for such a force and the United States' attempt to dominate the Western alliance by being the only nuclear power in it.[41]

The Chinese have made it clear that their presentation of the contradictions within the NATO alliance includes arguments that apply equally to Sino-Soviet differences. There have been veiled suggestions in Sino-Soviet polemics that the Chinese resisted Soviet proposals for cooperation in military nuclear affairs that would have involved stationing Soviet nuclear forces under Soviet control on Chinese territory. For example, the Chinese charged that "in 1958 the leadership of CPSU put forward unreasonable demands designed to bring China under Soviet military control. These unreasonable demands were rightly and firmly rejected by the Chinese Government."[42] The Chinese went on to declare that soon after this, the Soviet Union tore up the alleged agreement on providing China with information on new technology. Details of Sino-Soviet disagreement on this point have not yet been clarified, but one can suggest, in view of the great attention the Chinese give to the Franco-American situation, that some sort of analogous debate has taken place.

In their first formal response to the nuclear test ban treaty—

[40] NCNA dispatch broadcast, July 24, 1963, at 14:38 GMT and at 12:30 GMT on the Peking Home Service (in BBC SWB, FE/1310/A1/1, July 26, 1963).

[41] The Chinese have also been influenced, however, by the great difficulties the French have had. In a sense, to cite the French experience highlights not only the analogous situation in the Western camp, but the inherent difficulties in resisting the pressures from the dominant nuclear power in *any* bloc. For an analysis of the French nuclear program, see Ciro Zoppo, "France as a Nuclear Power," in Rosecrance (ed.), *The Dispersion of Nuclear Weapons*, pp. 113–56.

[42] "The Origin and Development of the Differences Between the Leadership of the CPSU and Ourselves—Comment on the Open Letter of the Central Committee of the CPSU," *People's Daily*, September 6, 1963. Translation in *Peking Review*, VI, No. 37 (September 13, 1963), 12. (Also in Griffith, *The Sino-Soviet Rift*, Document 10, p. 399.)

in which they proposed the complete prohibition and destruction of nuclear weapons—the Chinese demonstrated their
opposition to Soviet as well as American efforts to dominate
the world by maintaining a nuclear monopoly:

> In the eyes of U.S. imperialism, the countries of the world are
> divided into two categories: those which possess nuclear weap-
> ons and those which do not. The few nuclear powers, as a
> matter of course, are the masters of the world, whereas the
> countries which do not possess nuclear weapons are, to quote
> Kennedy, irresponsible and unstable, so that they are by no
> means qualified to possess nuclear weapons, nor can they have
> any say in the matter. In other words, those countries which do
> not possess nuclear weapons and the broad masses of people
> of the world must be left for ever to the tender mercies of
> others, and doomed to be the object of nuclear blackmail and
> nuclear threats.
>
> To speak frankly, if in this matter in international relations
> the principle followed is righteousness and justice and not
> tyranny and brute force, then no nuclear power has any right
> to dictate to any non-nuclear power—it has only the duty to
> submit itself to the demand of the people of all countries of
> the world for the complete prohibition and thorough destruc-
> tion of nuclear weapons.
>
> There are more than 130 countries in the world. All coun-
> tries, big or small, nuclear or non-nuclear, are equal. It is
> absolutely impermissible for two or three countries to brandish
> their nuclear weapons at will, issue orders and commands, and
> lord it over in the world as self-ordained nuclear overlords,
> while the overwhelming majority of countries are expected to
> kneel and obey orders meekly, as if they were nuclear slaves.[43]

Clearly, the Peking regime has concluded that in order to
have influence equal to the Soviet Union's within the socialist
camp, China must develop her own nuclear capability. It has
concluded, from the Soviet pressures to prevent them from

---

43 "People of the World, Unite! Strive for the Complete Prohibition and
Thorough Destruction of Nuclear Weapons!" *People's Daily*, August 2, 1963.
Translation in *Peking Review*, VI, No. 32 (August 9, 1963), 8.

developing such a capability as well as from the corresponding efforts by the United States to halt diffusion of nuclear power within the capitalist camp, that in fact nuclear weapons are an important source of intra-alliance power. Their suppositions are probably correct. China's influence within the international Communist movement may be expected to increase because of her detonation of a nuclear bomb and the fall of Khrushchev. The change of leadership in the Soviet Union leaves Mao as the outstanding figure in the international Communist movement. The Asian Communist parties are likely to be drawn even more firmly into the Chinese camp and more Communist parties may move into a neutral position—seeking to end the rift between the two great powers.

Supporting Wars of National Liberation

Closely related to China's desire for nuclear weapons to increase her influence within the Communist camp is the feeling that the Soviet Union has not used her nuclear power adequately in the support of wars of national liberation. This theme emerges quite clearly in the "Detonation Statement":

> The Chinese people firmly support the struggles for liberation waged by all oppressed nations and the people of the world. We are convinced that, by relying on their own struggles and also through mutual aid, the peoples of the world will certainly win victory.
>
> The mastering of the nuclear weapons by China is a great encouragement to the revolutionary peoples of the world in their struggles and a great contribution to the cause of defending world peace.

The Chinese do not believe that nuclear weapons can be used directly in wars of national liberation. On the contrary, in fact, they argue that neither the imperialist countries nor those engaged in a war of liberation can use nuclear weapons. The way in which the war is fought, including the intermingling of forces of both sides, makes the use of such weapons inappropriate.[44] This is the area in which the Chinese believe that it is the loyalty of men that is important and not a particular weapons system. Nevertheless, the Chinese believe that the Soviet Union is unwilling to support national-liberation wars and hence that they must take on this task, one they can assume more effectively if they are a nuclear power.

Chinese Hegemony in Asia

A fourth Chinese motivation for acquiring nuclear weapons, but one the Chinese are most reluctant to discuss, is their feeling that nuclear weapons would increase China's ability to establish hegemony in Asia. Chinese actions after the detonation of their nuclear bomb suggest that Peking is unlikely to try to resort to explicit nuclear blackmail or overt threats. Rather, the Chinese will try—by their nuclear detonation and their developing nuclear capability—to remind the countries of Asia of the presence of a major military power with whom they must come to terms. The Chinese realize that being the only Asian nuclear power would substantially increase China's prestige among Asian elites and would strengthen those such as Prince Sihanouk of Cambodia and General Ne Win of Burma who feel that the small nations of Asia must make their peace with Peking. In other words, a nuclear force will simply reinforce their conventional military power and their ability to support wars of national liberation, by enabling China to make *implicit* threats of military action against her neighbors while depending on political moves to bring these nations into her orbit. There seems to be no situation in which the employment of nuclear weapons would actually be

[44] "Two Different Lines on the Question of War and Peace—Comment on the Open Letter of the Central Committee of the CPSU [V]," *Peking Review*, November 22, 1963, p 13. (Also in Griffith, *op. cit.*, Document 16.)

contemplated by the Chinese or would, in fact, be useful in expanding Chinese influence.

THE 1958 TAIWAN STRAITS CRISIS

The Chinese have upbraided the Russians for monopolizing nuclear weapons and using them improperly in several past crises. After the Cuban missile crisis, they accused the Russians of the twin evils of adventurism and capitulationism.[45] They have also had several spirited exchanges on the part that Soviet nuclear weapons played in the Taiwan Straits crisis of 1958. These exchanges are significant because they highlight the questions of whether Soviet nuclear weapons would be available to support China's policies as well as to defend her against nuclear blackmail and, from the Chinese perspective, to pursue the correct line for international Communism. Secondarily, the exchanges shed light on the continuing dispute over Chinese strategy in the 1958 Taiwan Straits crisis and the nature of Sino-Soviet relations at that time.[46]

The first reference to the 1958 crisis in the public polemics of the Sino-Soviet rift came on January 8, 1963, when the Soviet Union declared:

> Who extinguished the raging flames of war in the Suez area in 1956 and compelled the Anglo-Franco-Israeli aggressors to retreat? Who prevented the imperialist-prepared invasion of Syria

[45] "Statement by the Spokesman of the Chinese Government—A Comment on the Soviet Government's Statement of August 21," *Peking Review,* September 6, 1963, p. 14.

[46] Most scholars of the 1958 crisis tend to support the later Chinese complaint that the Soviet Union failed to provide timely support for the Chinese adventure. See in particular John R. Thomas, "Soviet Behaviour in the Quemoy Crisis of 1958," *Orbis,* VI, No. 1 (Spring, 1962), 38–64; Zagoria, *The Sino-Soviet Conflict,* pp. 219–21; and Hsieh, *Communist China's Strategy in the Nuclear Era,* pp. 119–30. It is my own view that in fact the Soviet Union did provide to the Chinese the kind of nuclear cooperation and protection that they desired. Both interpretations can undoubtedly draw added evidence from the material that follows. In any event, whatever the actual historical facts, it is clear that for both sides the crisis provides a useful symbol for discussing the Chinese-Soviet nuclear relationship.

in 1957? *Who prevented war in the Middle East and in the Taiwan Straits in 1958?* This was done by the Soviet Union, by all the countries of the socialist camp, by the peace-loving forces. It was they and, above all, the might and vigorous actions of the U.S.S.R. that compelled the imperialist warmongers to retreat.[47] [Italics added.]

The Chinese did not at that time respond to the Soviet remarks, and the next reference to the crisis did not come until August 6 and 7, 1963, at the World Conference Against Atomic and Hydrogen Bombs in Hiroshima. In what the Japanese News Agency, Kyodo, described as a bitter exchange, the Soviet delegate, Zhukov, declared that to accuse the Soviet Union of betraying the people of the world was only to serve the purposes of imperialism. He asked the Chinese, "Was it not Russia that saved Communist China from the Taiwan Straits crisis?" According to the Tass dispatch of the meeting, he remarked that he could only express surprise that some speakers had insisted upon an all-or-nothing approach:

Pointing to the danger in such statements, the head of the Soviet delegation criticised the argument that . . . the American imperialists could create a climate of opinion that would prevent other socialist countries from possessing nuclear arms and thereby to deprive the socialist camp of the possibility of strengthening its power to resist blackmail by the U.S.A. G. Zhukov then gave examples of how the Soviet Union's nuclear strength had been completely and undividedly put at the service of the socialist camp. So it had been in September 1959 [*sic*], at the time of a sharp increase in tension in the region of the Taiwan Straits. . . .[48]

"Comrade Chu Tzu-chi is a responsible man who represents the C.P.R.—a socialist country, an ally bound to us by a treaty

[47] "Strengthen the Unity of the Communist Movement for the Triumph of Peace and Socialism," *Pravda*, January 7, 1963. Translation in *New Times* (Moscow), No. 2 (January 15, 1963). (Reprinted from same source in Dallin, *Diversity in International Communism*, Document 107, p. 734.)

[48] Kyodo press release, August 7, 1963.

of friendship, alliance and mutual aid, a country which, as I have already said, we have more than once saved from attempts at aggression by Taiwan. We then said bluntly that we would use atomic weapons to defend China."[49]

On the following day, according to NCNA, the Chinese delegate attacked the Soviet delegate's statement as "preposterous." He declared that in the past the Chinese people had relied mainly on their own strength and that the Soviet statement about having protected China with nuclear weapons was an insult to the Chinese people. He referred specifically to the Chinese civil war, the Korean War, and the Cuban crisis, but did not mention the Taiwan Straits incident.[50]

The first mention of the 1958 crisis in formal statements of the two governments on the nuclear test ban came in the Soviet Union's statement of August 21, 1963:

It cannot be effaced from the memory of the peoples that at the most critical moments, when aggressive circles brought the world to the brink of war, the Soviet Union has without hesitation applied all its international weight, its military might to stay the aggressor's hand raised over any country, whether small or big, geographically distant or close to us. This was the case at the time of the Suez crisis, this was the case during the events concerned with Syria and Iraq in 1958. *This was the case during the tense period in the Taiwan Strait—and the Chinese leaders and the Chinese people certainly remember it.* [Italics added.] This was also the case during the crisis in the Caribbean Sea, when the Soviet Union protected revolutionary Cuba with its nuclear rocket might. Maybe the Chinese leaders regard all these as minutes of "tranquillity." But it can be said outright that nobody else will agree with them. These steps by the Soviet Government were also an expression of genuine proletarian internationalism, not the kind which Peking likes

[49] Tass dispatch, August 6, 1963, in Russian (available, as is the Kyodo press release, in BBC SWB, FE/1320/C2/4–5, August 8, 1963).

[50] NCNA broadcast, August 6, 1963, at 14:00 GMT and Peking Home Service broadcast at 16:00 GMT (in BBC SWB, FE/1320/C2/3, August 8, 1963).

to talk about and which is backed by *nothing but noisy slogans and paper resolutions.*[51]

In their answer to this statement, the Chinese denied the Soviet interpretation of the Taiwan Straits events:

It is especially ridiculous that the Soviet statement also gives all the credit to Soviet nuclear weapons for the Chinese people's victory in smashing the armed provocations of U.S. imperialism in the Taiwan Straits in 1958. The Soviet paper *Krasnaya Zvezda* even said on August 25, 1963, "The nuclear might of the Soviet Union, the very country which has now been abused by the slanderers of Peking, had saved millions of Chinese from nuclear death and defended the sovereignty, security and independence of their country."

What were the facts? In August and September of 1958, the situation in the Taiwan Straits was indeed very tense as a result of the aggression and provocations by the U.S. imperialists. The Soviet leaders expressed their support for China on September 7 and 19 respectively. Although at that time the situation in the Taiwan Straits was tense, there was no possibility that a nuclear war would break out and no need for the Soviet Union to support China with its nuclear weapons. It was only when they were clear that this was the situation that the Soviet leaders expressed their support for China.

We have not forgotten and will not forget the support which the Soviet people have given to China on the question of Taiwan over a long period.[52]

The Chinese went on to declare, however, that Khrushchev, in October, 1959, after visiting the United States, had suggested to them that it might be necessary to accept the detachment of Taiwan from China for a long period. According to the Chinese, Khrushchev suggested that China accept the occupation of Taiwan by the United States, as the Soviet

[51] "Statement of the Soviet Government," *Peking Review*, September 6, 1963, p. 21. (Also in Griffith, *The Sino-Soviet Rift*, Document 8.)

[52] "A Statement by the Spokesman of the Chinese Government—A Comment on the Soviet Government's Statement of August 21."

Union had recognized the occupation of much Russian territory by foreign governments after the Russian Revolution.
The Chinese now charged that this had been to ask them to
accept the American scheme for "two Chinas" and reported
that "this absurd view was of course rebutted and rejected by
China, whereupon the Soviet leader made a series of speeches
hinting that China was 'craving for war like a cock for a fight,'
and, like Trotsky, wanted 'neither peace nor war,' etc."[53]

In their reply to the Peking statement, the Soviet Union
attempted to meet the charges. They declared first that Khrushchev had simply suggested there might be peaceful as well
as military ways to liberate Taiwan and that Russia had con-
tinually opposed any "two-China" situation. They rebutted
specifically the charges concerning the events of 1958:

> The Soviet Union has more than once proved by deeds its
> loyalty to its duty as an ally in relation to fraternal countries,
> including China. Who does not remember, for instance, that
> when a dangerous situation arose in the area of the Taiwan
> Strait in 1958, the Soviet government warned the President of
> the United States that it would regard an attack on the People's
> Republic of China as an attack on the Soviet Union and that if
> the aggressor used nuclear weapons, the Soviet Union would
> use its own nuclear rocket weapons to defend China.
>
> During those anxious days the Chinese leadership was grate-
> ful for the effective Soviet support and duly appreciated the
> role of the Soviet Union in ensuring the security of the Peo-
> ple's Republic of China. A letter from the Central Committee
> of the Communist Party of China of October 15, 1958, signed
> by Mao Tse-tung, said: "We are deeply touched by your bound-
> less devotion to the principles of Marxism-Leninism and inter-
> nationalism. On behalf of all the comrades who are members
> of the Communist Party of China, I convey heartfelt grati-
> tude . . ." [Ellipses appeared in Soviet statement.]
>
> After that, the letter continued as follows: "We are fully
> confident that should the events on Taiwan resolve themselves

[53] *Loc. cit.*

into a war between China and the United States, the Soviet Union will unfailingly render assistance to us with all its strength. Actually, in our struggle with the Americans, we have already now received powerful support from the Soviet Union." . . . Now that the critical days of the Taiwan crisis are behind us, the Chinese government is claiming the direct opposite.[54]

In November, the Chinese again denied that Soviet nuclear weapons had played a major role in the crisis and argued rather that Chinese action had permitted the Russians to remain outside the conflict:

The Chinese Communist Party is firmly opposed to a "head-on clash" between the Soviet Union and the United States, and not in words only. In deeds too it has worked hard to avert direct armed conflict between them. Examples of this are the Korean War against U.S. aggression in which we fought side by side with the Korean comrades and *our struggle against the United States in the Taiwan Straits.* We ourselves preferred to shoulder the heavy sacrifices necessary and stood in the first line of defence of the socialist camp so that the Soviet Union might stay in the second line.[55] [Italics added]

Soviet analysts continue to argue that the Soviet nuclear forces had been necessary and sufficient:

All the peoples now realize that at the most critical moments the Soviet Union has never wavered in throwing the full weight of its international authority and military might to tip the scales and stay the aggressor's hand about to fall on any country, big or small. Such was the case during the Caribbean crisis, *in the period of tension in the Taiwan Strait,* during the Anglo-French-Israeli aggression, and during the 1958 events in the Middle East, when the Soviet Union used its nuclear rocket might to shield Socialist Cuba, *to avert aggression against the*

[54] "A Reply to Peking—Soviet Government Statement," *Soviet Booklet No. 122,* pp. 15–16. (Also in Griffith, *op. cit.,* Document 12.)

[55] "Two Different Lines on the Question of War and Peace—Comment on the Open Letter of the Central Committee of the CPSU [V]," *Peking Review,* November 22, 1963, pp. 12–13.

Chinese People's Republic, and safeguard the independence and freedom of Egypt, Syria and Iraq.[56] [Italics added]

In 1964, in a radio broadcast from Russia, the Chinese people were told that:

In the autumn of 1958, when the United States massed its troops in the Taiwan Strait and the danger of a large-scale military clash was imminent, Khrushchev, chairman of the U.S.S.R. Council of Ministers, in his letter of 10 September 1958 to U.S. President Eisenhower pointed out: "China is not alone and has faithful friends who are ready to come to its aid should China be attached [sic] because the security of People's China is closely related with that of the U.S.S.R."

The Soviet Government warned: "Any attack on the C.P.R., the great friend, ally, and neighboring country of the U.S.S.R., will be considered as an attack on the U.S.S.R. The U.S.S.R. which is loyal to its obligation will do its best to maintain security of the two countries and safeguard the interests of peace in the Far East and the world in close cooperation with People's China."

Ulbricht, first secretary of the SED Central Committee, said on 9 September 1958 that the G.D.R. people deeply sympathized with the Chinese people who are struggling for justice. On 8 September 1958, the American ambassador to Czechoslovakia was summoned at the Czechoslovak foreign office and was told that the presence of U.S. troops in the Taiwan Strait and U.S. intervention in China's internal affairs were termed aggressive action against the C.P.R. The Czechoslovak Government emphatically pointed out that it supported the Chinese people's legitimate rights. China highly praised the Soviet support and its unfailing loyalty to proletarian internationalism and obligations to allies.[57]

56 I. Glagolev and V. Larionov, "Soviet Defence Might and Peaceful Coexistence," *International Affairs* (Moscow), XI (November, 1963), 29.

57 Radio broadcast in Mandarin from Moscow to China, second in a series by Professor Kapitsa, "The Chinese People Have Their Faithful Friends," 13:00 GMT, October 2, 1964.

Regardless of the actual state of affairs in 1958, it is clear that both Communist China and the Soviet Union are attempting to use the incident to prove their points in the current dispute. The latter is suggesting that China does not need nuclear weapons because Russia will always come to her aid. The Chinese, for their part, question whether the Soviets have in fact helped them and, even more, express their conviction that Soviet nuclear weapons are not likely to be available for Chinese offensive action, including the taking of Taiwan.

CHINESE POLICY ON THE TEST BAN TREATY AND ON DISARMAMENT

Prior to the 1963 Moscow negotiations on the test ban, the Chinese had generally supported Soviet proposals to abolish nuclear weapons, but had made it clear that they would not sign any treaty unless they participated in the negotiations.[58] After the test ban treaty was signed in June, 1963, they vigorously attacked the Russians for agreeing to it and frankly disclaimed any intention of adhering to the document. The Chinese have discussed at great length their reasons for opposing the treaty. One of these, their need to develop their own nuclear capability, has already been examined. It is also important to note that perhaps the major reason for their agitation about the actual signing of the treaty was that they foresaw the political effect it would have in Asia: A test ban treaty would diminish the political value of their explosion of a nuclear weapon; indeed, it had already served to brand

[58] NCNA press release, January 21, 1960. Translated in SCMP, No. 2185, p. 4; and *The New York Times,* April 11, 1960. See also Ciro E. Zoppo, "The Accession of Other Nations to the Nuclear Test Ban" (The RAND Corporation, RM-2730-ARPA, March, 1961); Alice Langley Hsieh, "The Chinese Genie: Peking's Role in the Nuclear Test Ban Negotiations" (The RAND Corporation, P-2022, June 20, 1960); and A. Doak Barnett, "The Inclusion of Communist China in an Arms Control Program," in Donald G. Brennan (ed.), *Arms Control, Disarmament and National Security* (New York: George Braziller, 1961), pp. 282–303.

them as outlaws interfering with the possibility of ending the atomic arms race.

Though the Chinese do not for obvious reasons allude to this reasoning, they present a suspiciously large number of other arguments against the nuclear test ban: that the treaty is an excuse for the Soviet Union not to share nuclear weapons with the Chinese; that it permits underground tests and hence will permit the United States to proceed with her development of tactical nuclear weapons; that it will provide a means of establishing a "two-China" situation; that it is not real disarmament; and, finally, that it is a form of *détente* between the United States and the Soviet Union. These points were all made when the test ban treaty was signed and reiterated after the Chinese detonation of an atomic device.

Perhaps the major theme is that the nuclear test ban treaty is looked upon by the Kremlin as an excuse not to share nuclear weapons with China. The Chinese argue, however, that the treaty will not prevent proliferation of nuclear weapons within the imperialist camp; in fact, they say, the United States is pressing ahead with its proposals for a multilateral force. In this connection, the Chinese maintain that the multilateral nuclear force is a disguised attempt to give nuclear weapons to Germany, an argument that is in marked contrast to the one they advance at other times—that it is an effort to perpetuate the American nuclear monopoly. Thus, while the Chinese were previously inclined to believe that the Russians genuinely wanted to forestall the spread of nuclear weapons to Germany and therefore felt that they could not give similar weapons to China, they now came to the conclusion that the "real aim of the Soviet leaders is to compromise with the United States in order to seek momentary ease and to maintain a monopoly of nuclear weapons and lord it over in the socialist camp."[59]

---

[59] "Statement by the Spokesman of the Chinese Government—A Comment on the Soviet Government's Statement of August 3," *Peking Review*, August 15, 1963, p. 13.

The Chinese charge that the Soviet Union has tried to "manacle" them—a term they frequently use in this regard—ever since 1959, when she broke the agreement to supply China with nuclear weapons. The Chinese also indicate that they made a number of representations to the Soviet Union to avoid any kind of test ban or other agreement that would commit the Soviets to a policy preventing the development of a Chinese nuclear capability. In September and October, 1962, and again in June, 1963, according to the Chinese, they sent notes to the Soviet Government expressing the hope that the Soviet Government would not accede to any agreement that would infringe on China's sovereign rights or that would appear to commit China to refrain from manufacturing nuclear weapons. After the treaty was signed, China's resentment was plain:

> We solemnly stated that we would not tolerate the conclusion, in disregard of China's opposition, of any sort of treaty between the Soviet Government and the United States which aimed at depriving the Chinese people of their right to take steps to resist the nuclear threats of U.S. imperialism, and that we would issue statements to make our position known.
>
> We hoped that after such earnest counsel from us, the Soviet leaders would rein in before reaching the precipice and would not render matters irretrievable. Unfortunately, they did not pay the slightest attention to our counsel. They finally concluded the treaty on the partial halting of nuclear tests with the United States and Britain, thereby attempting to bring pressure to bear on China and force her into commitments.
>
> The whole course of events amounts to this: First the Soviet Government tried to subdue China and curry favour with U.S. imperialism by discontinuing assistance to China. Then it put forward all sorts of untenable arguments in an attempt to induce China to abandon its solemn stand. Failing in all this, it has brazenly ganged up with the imperialist bandits in exerting pressure on China.[60]

The Chinese view the test ban, and the Soviet Union's will-

[60] *Loc. cit.*

ingness to try to prevent them from acquiring nuclear weapons, as the price the Russians are prepared to pay for *détente* with the West. They cite a number of Western sources to show that the United States sought the test ban in an effort to divide Russia from China and to halt the spread of nuclear weapons to China. Over and beyond their resentment at being "sold out" by the Russians, and their opposition to any real *détente*—which they recognize would imply a Soviet decision not to give nuclear weapons to China—the Chinese appear to abhor the whole idea of accommodating "imperialists." They argued publicly before the signing of the test ban treaty and argue now that *détente* would be dangerous because it would create a false sense of peace. In doing so, the Chinese were able to draw on previous Russian statements:

> What is of more serious consequence is that to cease nuclear tests according to the U.S. proposal may give rise to a false sense of security among the peoples and lull their vigilance in their struggle to defend peace. In September 1961 the Soviet Government correctly pointed out in its memorandum on nuclear weapon tests to the 16th Session of the U.N. General Assembly, "It became clear that the conclusion of a separate treaty on discontinuing nuclear tests at a time when the Western powers were pursuing a reckless arms race could only create a general illusion that something was being done to prevent a nuclear war, whereas the Western powers were actually pushing matters precisely to such a war.
>
> "The conclusion of a treaty on discontinuing nuclear tests in such an atmosphere and in isolation from a programme for general and complete disarmament could only give the peoples of the world a false sense of security, and would act as a kind of drug to lull their vigilance on the question of the preservation of peace."
>
> Thus, if this U.S. fraud should succeed, the pursuit of nuclear blackmail and the danger of a nuclear war would not be reduced but would increase greatly.[61]

61 *People's Daily*, July 19, 1963. Translation in *Peking Review*, VI, No. 30 (July 26, 1963), 47–48.

When their advice was ignored and the treaty signed, the Chinese asserted precisely that the treaty had now created a false sense of security against which there had to be reaction.

The Chinese have argued that only complete and total nuclear disarmament is acceptable and that anything less, in the form of a test ban treaty, can only be dangerous to the forces of peace. Thus the first Chinese reaction to the test ban treaty was a statement "advocating the complete, thorough, total and resolute prohibition and destruction of nuclear weapons; proposing a conference of the government heads of all countries of the world." The Chinese proposal, which was later reiterated in a letter from Premier Chou En-lai to all heads of government (and again in a statement following the detonation of the Chinese nuclear device), first attacked the three-environment test ban treaty as a "fraud" and then urged nations to subscribe to the following articles:

(1) All countries in the world, both nuclear and non-nuclear, solemnly declare that they will prohibit and destroy nuclear weapons completely, thoroughly, totally and resolutely. Concretely speaking, they will not use nuclear weapons, nor export, nor import, nor manufacture, nor test, nor stockpile them; and they will destroy all the existing nuclear weapons and their means of delivery in the world, and disband all the existing establishments for the research, testing and manufacture of nuclear weapons in the world.

(2) In order to fulfil the above undertakings step by step, the following measures shall be adopted first:

a. Dismantle all military bases, including nuclear bases, on foreign soil, and withdraw from abroad all nuclear weapons and their means of delivery.

b. Establish a nuclear-weapon–free zone of the Asian and Pacific region, including the United States, the Soviet Union, China and Japan; a nuclear-weapon–free zone of Central Europe; a nuclear-weapon–free zone of Africa; and a nuclear-weapon–free zone of Latin America. The countries possessing nuclear weapons shall undertake due obligations with regard to each of the nuclear-weapon–free zones.

c. Refrain from exporting and importing in any form nuclear weapons and technical data for their manufacture.

d. Cease all nuclear tests, including underground nuclear tests.

(3) A conference of the government heads of all the countries of the world shall be convened to discuss the question of the complete prohibition and thorough destruction of nuclear weapons and the question of taking the above-mentioned four measures in order to realize step by step the complete prohibition and thorough destruction of nuclear weapons.[62]

This constitutes the current Chinese position on disarmament. Disarmament must include the destruction of all nuclear weapons in the world, and this must be begun by creating nuclear-weapon–free zones. The Chinese have included Russia in the Pacific zone they propose, in which they have consistently insisted the United States must participate. It is not clear whether the Chinese have anything definite in mind in this regard—whether they are implying that part of the United States and part of the Soviet Union in the Pacific area should not have nuclear weapons in it, or whether all of the Soviet Union and all of the United States should be part of any proposed Asian nuclear-weapon–free zone. Either way, the proposals undoubtedly are designed for propaganda purposes—to counteract the adverse effects of China's rejection of the nuclear test ban treaty and her nuclear tests—and are not meant to be taken as negotiable proposals.

Following their detonation of a nuclear bomb, the Chinese gave even greater emphasis to a ban on the use of nuclear weapons. They made a unilateral commitment never to use nuclear weapons first, pointed out that the United States had never made such a commitment, and called for an international agreement. In a second letter to all heads of government in 1964, Chou En-lai made the following proposal:

62 Translation of the statement in *Peking Review*, VI, No. 31 (August 2, 1963), 8; translation of the text of the letter in *Peking Review*, VI, No. 32 (August 9, 1963), 7. (Reprinted from NCNA, August 4, 1963, in Griffith, *op. cit.*, Document 5, p. 330.)

That a summit conference of all the countries of the world be convened to discuss the question of the complete prohibition and thorough destruction of nuclear weapons, and that as the first step, the summit conference should reach an agreement to the effect that the nuclear powers and those countries which may soon become nuclear powers undertake not to use nuclear weapons, neither to use them against non-nuclear countries and nuclear-free zones, nor against each other.[63]

The only non-Communist regime in Asia that refused to sign the test ban treaty was Cambodia. In a statement of September 20, 1963, the Cambodian head of state, Prince Sihanouk, according to NCNA, declared:

We have not signed the Moscow treaty on the prohibition of nuclear tests because we do not want to sign on an illusory promise to peace. . . . Since the countries who have signed are free to carry on underground tests, the menace to peace remains and the future of humanity continues to be in a tragically precarious state. The menace is still there. . . . China, also, did not sign the treaty because it stands for a complete and genuine ban on all nuclear tests. . . . We are happy that our views and those of the views of the greatly friendly republic— the People's Republic of China—are the same. . . . We prefer to be with China alone than with a multitude of countries, who in case of danger, would leave us in the cold. . . . Our international policy is based on neutrality. But should we be obliged one day to choose between China and the others, we would, without hesitation, choose to be on the side of the People's Republic of China, for she alone would take the trouble to fight on our side in case of aggressions from our neighbours.[64]

On the other hand, Burma did sign the test ban treaty. The Burmese Government noted that it represented a significant step toward a total ban on nuclear tests in all places, and ex-

[63] "Premier Chou Cables Government Heads of the World," *Peking Review*, VII, No. 43 (October 23, 1964), 6.

[64] NCNA broadcast, September 21, 1963, at 15:59 GMT (in BBC SWB, FE/1362/C/1, September 26, 1963).

pressed the belief that it would lead to the total abolition of all weapons capable of the destruction of mankind. The statement welcoming the treaty concluded: "It will be a great contribution toward world peace should those countries, which already possess or soon will possess atomic weapons, promote this spirit."[65]

Two other minor themes have run through China's objections to the nuclear test ban: that the treaty helps to promote the "two-China plot" because the "Chiang Kai-shek clique" was permitted to sign it (the Chinese attacked the Russians for not objecting to the Kuomintang signature, and wondered whether this did not herald Russian acceptance of a two-China situation[66]); and that since it does not ban underground tests, the treaty permits the United States to continue the research on tactical nuclear weapons which, under her strategy of flexible response, are becoming more important and a serious menace to Chinese security. By not prohibiting underground tests, the Chinese declared the tripartite treaty in fact legalized such tests and made it easier for the United States to develop tactical nuclear weapons in preparation for limited nuclear wars:

> At present, the United States is eagerly seeking to develop tactical nuclear weapons. It intends to use tactical nuclear weapons in local wars in order to deal with non-nuclear socialist and other peace-loving countries and people, and in particular to deal with the Asian, African and Latin American countries and people which are subjected to oppression and aggression.
> If this U.S. imperialist scheme should be allowed to succeed,

[65] Rangoon Home Service broadcast, July 29, 1963, at 13:15 GMT (in BBC SWB, FE/1315/A1/5, August 1, 1963). Several other Asian and African states both signed the test ban treaty and responded favorably to the Chinese proposal. See, for example, response of Sierra Leone, reported by NCNA in English, September 6, 1963 (in SCMP, No. 3057, September 11, 1963, p. 38); and of Pakistan, reported by NCNA in English, September 20, 1963 (in SCMP, No. 3067, September 25, 1963, pp. 43–44).

[66] NCNA broadcast, September 11, 1963, at 19:47 GMT, and Peking Home Service broadcast at 22:30 GMT (in BBC SWB, FE/1351/C2/2–3).

and if U.S. imperialism should be permitted to win in one local war after another and so change the international balance of forces, it would in turn definitely increase the danger of a total nuclear war. This situation cannot but rouse the people's serious vigilance.[67]

In expressing their opposition to the nuclear test ban treaty and also in suggesting the conditions under which they would be prepared to abandon their nuclear program—clearly unacceptable to the West—the Chinese laid the groundwork that they used in justifying their own nuclear tests and their development of nuclear weapons. They will undoubtedly continue to advocate a ban on being the first to use nuclear weapons and other measures leading to nuclear disarmament —thereby attempting to appeal to groups that favor disarmament, rather than to sign any agreements with the United States.

[67] "Statement by the Spokesman of the Chinese Government—A Comment on the Soviet Government's Statement of August 3."

3

China's Nuclear Potential[1]

W HILE CHINA'S INTEREST IN
acquiring nuclear weapons probably dates back to the early
1950's, the Chinese Communists appear to have launched
their nuclear weapons' development program only in 1957.
In May, 1957, they set up an Institute of Atomic Energy and
in October, apparently, signed an agreement under which the
Russians agreed to assist them in the production of nuclear
weapons.

[1] In addition to press reports based on background briefings by Washington
officials, this chapter draws on the following sources: Leonard Beaton and
John Maddox, *The Spread of Nuclear Weapons* (New York: Frederick A.
Praeger, 1962); Arnold Kramish, *The Peaceful Atom in Foreign Policy* (New
York: Harper & Row, for the Council on Foreign Relations, 1963); Frank E.
Armbruster *et al.*, "The Political and Military Posture of Communist China,"
in "A Framework for the 1965–1975 Strategic Debate" (Hudson Institute,
HI-202-RR, August 9, 1963), Appendix A; T. Y. Wu, "Nuclear Physics," in
Sidney H. Gould (ed.), *Sciences in Communist China* (American Association
for the Advancement of Science, 1961); John A. Berberet, "Science and Technology in Communist China" (General Electric Company, TEMPO, RM-
60TMP-72, December 8, 1960); George A. Modelski, *Atomic Energy in the*

The first public admission by a Chinese official of Peking's intention to develop nuclear weapons came in 1958, when Foreign Minister Chen Yi told German press correspondents that China would have nuclear weapons.[2] Shortly afterward, in the first official statement, the Commander-in-Chief of the Chinese Air Force, Liu Ya-lou, wrote, "China's working class and scientists will certainly be able to make the most up-to-date aircraft and atomic bombs in the not distant future. . . . By that time . . . we can use atomic weapons and guided missiles . . . in coping with the enemies who dare to invade our country."[3]

After that, Chou En-lai, Chen Yi, and other leaders made it unmistakably clear that China was determined to develop a nuclear capability. The Chinese nuclear test of October, 1964, near Lake Lop Nor in Sinkiang Province, indicates that at least since 1957, the Chinese have given very high priority to the development of nuclear weapons.

The production of nuclear weapons and delivery systems requires sophisticated industrial technology and the expenditure of large sums of money. It requires the development of fissional material either in the form of plutonium or uranium 238, of facilities for handling the fissional material and turning it into deliverable bombs, and of delivery systems in the form of missiles or airplanes. Such a program requires at least several theoretical physicists and many more applied physi-

---

Communist Bloc (Melbourne: Melbourne University Press for the Australian National University, 1959); Alice Langley Hsieh, "China's Secret Military Papers: Military Doctrine and Strategy," China Quarterly, No. 18 (April–June, 1964), pp. 79–99; Christoph Hohenemser, "The Nth Country Problem Today," in Seymour Melman (ed.), Disarmament: Its Politics and Economics (Boston: American Academy of Arts and Sciences, 1962), pp. 238–76; Chalmers Johnson, "China's 'Manhattan Project,'" The New York Times Magazine, October 25, 1964; pp. 23, 117–19; The New York Times, October 29, 1963, p. 14.

[2] Die Welt (Hamburg), and Stuttgarter Zeitung, May 10, 1958. See also Klaus Mehnert, Peking and Moscow (New York: Putnam's, 1963), p. 436.

[3] "Seriously Study Mao Tse-tung's Military Thinking," Liberation Army Newspaper, May 23, 1958; translated in SCMP, No. 1900, November 24, 1958.

cists, engineers, and other technicians. There are two basic routes that China or any other country can follow in attempting to carry out this program. The first, which is the route Britain and France followed, involves the construction of atomic reactors that use natural uranium to produce weapons-grade plutonium. The alternative, which the French are also using, is to build a gaseous diffusion plant to separate uranium and yield weapons-grade uranium 238. A nuclear reactor capable of producing enough fissional material for one weapon per year would cost about $50 million.[4] The gaseous diffusion plant which the French are now building at Pierrelette, in Provence, is estimated to cost approximately $1 billion.[5]

This is indeed a high cost, but it is unlikely that the Chinese, in building both a diffusion plant and at least two reactors, have found their nuclear-weapons *development* program in the last analysis to have been detrimental to their rate of economic growth. The Chinese Gross National Product (GNP) was estimated to be $35–45 billion in 1957.[6] Their nuclear-weapons program has probably cost them the equivalent of approximately 2 per cent of their GNP and could be drawn from a defense budget of more than $2.3 billion.[7] Electric power, which is used in large quantities in a nuclear development program, particularly in the operation of a diffusion plant, is currently in excess supply in China because of overproduction during the Great Leap Forward in 1958–59. Thus, at least until they start producing large quantities of fissionable material or many delivery systems, the major cost will be in training scientists and engineers and putting them

4 Beaton and Maddox, *op. cit.*, p. 22.

5 Kramish, *op. cit.*, p. 14.

6 T. C. Liu and K. C. Yeh, "The Economy of the Chinese Mainland: National Income and Economic Development, 1933–1959" (The RAND Corporation, RM-3519-PR, 1953). I am indebted to Dwight Perkins for several of the economic calculations made in this chapter.

7 *The New York Times*, April 22, 1959, p. 1.

to work. Requiring perhaps 2,000 engineers and 750 scientists for research and development, and an equal number for production of materials, the Chinese program would use only 3.4 per cent of available Chinese scientists and engineers in the relevant fields. But this figure substantially underates the manpower costs, since the Chinese have had to use many of their best scientists and engineers—particularly from the fields of chemical and electrical engineering, which have been lagging in China.

The Chinese are known to have several first-rate nuclear scientists. The elite group of physicists includes Chou Pei-Yuan, Wang Kan-chang (who was educated in Germany before World War II and at the University of California at Berkeley after the war, and who is believed to be in charge of the nuclear-weapons program), Tsien San-tsiang (who once collaborated with the French atomic scientist Joliot-Curie and is now director of the Chinese Institute of Atomic Energy), and Tsien's wife, Peng Tse-fri. Some 950 Chinese scientists had been enrolled in or graduated from the Dubna Institute for nuclear research in the Soviet Union.

Besides financial cost and scientific manpower, the question of materials and technology must also be considered. Chinese nuclear scientists have at their disposal large deposits of uranium in Chinese territory, particularly in Sinkiang, and they have the capability to extract the uranium and prepare it for use. The Chinese are known to be short of the nickel and chromium needed for piping in a separation plant, but they have imported sufficient quantities of both materials. They are reported to be producing lithium, which is apparently needed for fusion weapons. Given fissionable material, therefore, the Chinese would not be expected to have had any difficulty in designing a bomb. Even if they had not received Soviet aid, there was public literature available that explains problems of simple bomb design. In fact, "a recipe for a bomb" was recently given in a study published for the Council on Foreign Relations.[8]

The Chinese have made public the existence of at least one nuclear reactor in the People's Republic; supplied by the Russians, it went into operation in September, 1958, and appears to be used for research purposes.[9] The Chinese also have two plutonium-producing weapons-grade reactors, located near Paotaw, in Inner Mongolia. One of the reactors at Paotaw is evidently a rather large one of perhaps 200 million watts that produces plutonium 239. Estimates of the productive capacity of these reactors made on the assumption that they used natural uranium indicated that they could produce enough plutonium for two low-yield nuclear devices a year. If, as it now seems likely, the reactors operate with some enriched uranium provided by the gaseous diffusion plant, their production is substantially greater.

The reported Chinese gaseous diffusion plant, near Lanchow, in northwest China, is powered by a huge hydroelectric installation built nearby at the Liu-Chie gorge on the Yellow River. This plant probably produced the enriched uranium used in the first Chinese nuclear device. It had previously been known that the Chinese had a diffusion plant, although before the analysis of the Chinese nuclear test had been made by the Atomic Energy Commission, it had been assumed that the plant was not in operation. The only alternative hypotheses are that the Chinese received or stole the material from the Russians or that they used a new technique, such as the gas-centrifuge method, for separating uranium. If, and it seems most unlikely, the Soviet Union was the source of the enriched uranium, the Chinese acquired the material by 1960 at the latest, and they would not have had any reason to wait to use it in a test. Other methods of producing uranium are, at least at present, more expensive and no less complicated

8 Kramish, *op. cit.*, pp. 10–27.
9 Beaton and Maddox, *op. cit.*, p. 124.

than the construction of a diffusion plant. Thus the most likely explanation is that the Chinese have an operating gaseous diffusion plant that is capable of producing a substantial number of uranium bombs per year, and that will substantially increase the efficiency of the plutonium reactors. With the ability to enrich uranium, the Chinese should be able to produce a fusion weapon in a few years.

Prior to the detonation of China's bomb, it had been generally assumed that the Chinese would choose the first of the two possible programs for acquiring nuclear power, that they would build reactors which, using natural uranium, produce weapons-grade plutonium. This assumption was based on the belief that the Chinese were not receiving large-scale Soviet assistance and that: (1) available public literature contains much more information on plutonium reactors than on the gaseous diffusion process; (2) technological problems are less great in the production of plutonium; (3) the cost of plutonium production may be somewhat lower; and (4) plutonium reactors produce electric power as a by-product, while the gaseous diffusion process uses vast quantities of electricity. Given these considerations, it is extremely unlikely that the Chinese undertook to build a gaseous diffusion plant without Russian aid. With such aid, however, the plant construction could have been justified on the grounds that the use of enriched uranium increased the reactors' productive capacity by an amount sufficient to justify the cost. In addition, the Chinese must have been aware that enriched uranium was highly desirable, if not absolutely necessary, to enable them to proceed with a fusion-weapons program. Once having decided to build a gaseous diffusion plant, the Chinese apparently had no choice but to build a large one: According to an official United States Government publication, "Gaseous diffusion plants are inherently of substantial capacity and require very large amounts of electrical power.[10]

10 United States Atomic Energy Commission, *Annual Report to Congress, 1960* (Washington, D.C.: U.S. Government Printing Office, 1961), p. 503.

The Chinese undoubtedly recognize that means of delivery are as important as the nuclear weapons themselves in an effective nuclear force. They are evidently giving the same priority to the development of a missile delivery system as to the development of nuclear warheads—a necessary development since the Chinese have yet to produce a single plane on their own, although they have assembled Soviet MIG 15's and MIG 17's from parts supplied by the Russians. These supplies have apparently dried up, and the Chinese are reported to be cannibalizing their existing military aircraft—i.e., using parts from some to keep others in flying condition.[11] In addition to these jets, the Chinese have some Soviet-supplied TU-4 bombers, and they may think that in a pinch they could carry their first nuclear weapons in these planes. They must recognize, however, that the planes will be close to complete obsolescence by the time they possess warheads (within perhaps three years) small enough to be carried in them.

The Chinese are known to maintain a missile research program headed by Dr. Chien Hsueh-shen, a former Professor of Jet Propulsion at the California Institute of Technology who was associated with American rocket development programs. (Dr. Chien returned to China from the United States in 1955.[12]) Also working on the program are Chien Wei-chang, who had been at the Jet Propulsion Laboratory of the California Institute of Technology too, and Wei Chung-hua, formerly of the Massachusetts Institute of Technology.

At some time in 1958, Peking probably decided to give priority to missile production, in the expectation of receiving Soviet assistance. *Pravda,* for example, indicated on May 18, 1958, that the Chinese were studying Soviet techniques so that they could launch their own satellites, and defectors from China indicated that the Chinese were working on rockets. The Chinese are reported to have an IRBM range near Chiu-

---

11 *The Christian Science Monitor,* February 21, 1964, p. 9.
12 *The New York Times,* October 17, 1964, p. 10.

chan,[13] and one observer has stated that the Chinese are testing missiles on 500- to 700-mile ranges.[14]

The Chinese themselves are no doubt aware of the long and
difficult road they will have to travel before they become a
real nuclear power. They have admitted these difficulties publicly, as well as in the guise of comment on the difficulties
encountered by the French in their nuclear program.[15] On
October 28, 1963, Vice-Premier Chen Yi told a group of Japanese newspapermen visiting Peking this story: Premier Khrushchev had once said, remarked Chen Yi, that the manufacture
of atomic weapons cost so much money that China might have
no money left to make trousers with. China, Chen Yi concluded, will have to manufacture the weapons with or without trousers.[16]

SOVIET NUCLEAR ASSISTANCE TO CHINA

Two major variables that have substantially affected the
timetable of Chinese nuclear development are Sino-Soviet relations and Soviet assistance to China's nuclear program.[17] To
what extent China can rely on Russia indefinitely for her nuclear protection, rather than seeking to develop her own capa-

13 Hsieh, "China's Secret Military Papers."
14 Statement by Robert Hotz, editor of *Aviation Week,* on a television program recorded May 27, 1963. Cited in Hsieh, "China's Secret Military Papers,"
p. 93 n.
15 See, for example, Peking Home Service broadcast, February 21, 1963, at
12:10 GMT (in BBC SWB, FE/1183/A1/2, February 23, 1963).
16 Dispatch of Japanese news agency *Kyodo,* October 28, 1963, evening edi-
tion; reported in *The New York Times,* October 29, 1963, pp. 1, 14.
17 For discussion of Soviet nuclear relations with China, see Raymond L.
Garthoff, "Sino-Soviet Military Relations," *Annals of the American Academy
of Political and Social Science,* CCCXLIX (September, 1963), 81–93; Alice
Langley Hsieh, *Communist China's Strategy in the Nuclear Era,* and "The
Sino-Soviet Nuclear Dialogue: 1963" (The RAND Corporation, P-2852, January,
1964); Harold P. Ford, "Modern Weapons and the Sino-Soviet Estrangement,"
China Quarterly, No. 18 (April–June, 1964), pp. 160–73; Thomas W. Wolfe,
Soviet Strategy at the Crossroads (Cambridge, Mass.: Harvard University
Press, 1964), pp. 216–24.

bility, is a question that, according to some observers, has divided the Chinese military and political hierarchy.[18]

In the early years of the regime, particularly at the time of the Korean War, the Chinese had had no choice but to depend on the Soviet Union for nuclear deterrence, but they have probably also, to a certain degree, doubted whether Russia would in fact come to their aid in the event of a nuclear attack from the United States. Nevertheless, their economic situation rendered the start of a nuclear program out of the question, although they laid the groundwork for it—in terms both of general industrial and scientific development and of the education of nuclear physicists and technicians.

There seems to be little doubt that, between 1957 and 1959, the Soviet Union supplied China with extensive assistance in the nuclear-weapons field. President Johnson stated the American Government's estimate that:

> At first, in the nineteen-fifties Russia helped the Chinese. This assistance in the spread of nuclear weapons may now be regarded with some dismay today in Moscow.
>
> We believe that this help was ended in 1960 as the quarrel among the Communists grew sharper. Soviet scientists and technicians left suddenly, with the blueprints under their arms. Unfinished facilities were left standing, and expected supplies were cut off.[19]

Chinese scientists worked at the Soviet-sponsored Nuclear Research Institute at Dubna in a cooperative research venture for which China apparently paid some 20 per cent of the cost.[20] In August, 1958, rumors circulated in Eastern Europe that the Soviet Union had agreed to supply China with nuclear weapons and missiles. (At least one story commenting on

[18] Hsieh, *Communist China's Strategy in the Nuclear Age,* where the available evidence on this question is examined in detail; the author argues that there has been a major and (until 1962) unresolved split on this question.

[19] Speech of October 18, text in *The New York Times,* October 19, 1964, p. 14.

[20] Beaton and Maddox, *op. cit.,* p. 42.

these rumors—in a *New York Times* dispatch from Moscow—was passed by Soviet censors.[21]) It is also known that the Soviet Union supplied the Chinese with an experimental atomic reactor that went into operation the next month.[22] In the summer of 1959, Khrushchev told Averell Harriman that Russia had shipped numerous rockets to China.[23] And, as was indicated above, the Chinese almost certainly received substantial aid (including, perhaps, needed but hard-to-produce pumps) in the construction of their gaseous diffusion plant.

These nuclear relations have produced sharp polemics between China and the Soviet Union. The Chinese have declared that they signed an agreement with the U.S.S.R. on "new technology for national defense" on October 15, 1957, which was unilaterally broken by the Russians on June 20, 1959, when they refused to provide the Chinese with "a sample of an atomic bomb and technical data concerning its manufacture."[24] The Soviets confirm the existence of some kind of an agreement on nuclear technology signed in 1957, but accuse the Chinese of "presenting the facts tendentiously and in a distorted light."[25] According to the American Government, the Soviet Union did give the Chinese assistance on their nuclear-weapons program and did not terminate it until 1960.[26] But it appears that after signing the agreement in 1957, the Soviet Union began to put limitations or conditions on the assistance they were willing to give.

In 1958, they made some request to the Chinese concerning

[21] *The New York Times*, August 18, 1958, p. 1.

[22] NCNA dispatch in English, September 27, 1958 (in SCMP, No. 1865, October 1, 1958, pp. 12–13).

[23] *Life*, July 13, 1959, 36.

[24] "Statement by the Spokesman of the Chinese Government—A Comment on the Soviet Government's Statement of August 3," *Peking Review*, August 15, 1963, p. 14. The Soviet Government characterized the formal Chinese note in which this charge was made as "slanderous and hostile" (*The New York Times*, August 22, 1963, p. 15).

[25] "Statement of the Soviet Government," August 21, 1963, *Peking Review*, September 6, 1963, p. 21.

[26] Speech by President Johnson, October 18, 1964.

nuclear weapons—perhaps for permission to place Soviet-controlled strategic missiles on Chinese territory—which the Chinese rejected.[27] At about the same time, apparently, they began their efforts to convince the Chinese that preventing the spread of nuclear weapons was in the interests of China and that they should therefore abandon their nuclear program and rely on the Soviet Union. Both privately and publicly to the Chinese, and in statements to American officials (prior to the Chinese detonation of a bomb), high Soviet officials deprecated Chinese nuclear developments and suggested that China was far from being a nuclear power. They also pointed out that China can possess only a very small nuclear capability and only at great expense to her economy; if the effort were to stimulate further spread of nuclear weapons, China's sacrifice would merely place her in an even less stable position.[28] The Chinese confirmed this Soviet position:

> Is not China very poor and backward? Yes, it is. The Soviet leaders say, how can the Chinese be qualified to manufacture nuclear weapons when they eat watery soup out of a common bowl and do not even have pants to wear?
>
> The Soviet leaders are perhaps too hasty in deriding China for its backwardness. They may or may not have judged right. But in any case, even if we Chinese people are unable to produce an atom bomb for a hundred years, we will neither crawl to the baton of the Soviet leaders nor kneel before the nuclear blackmail of the U.S. imperialists.
>
> The Soviet statement says that if China were to produce two or three atom bombs, the imperialists would aim many more atom bombs at China. This is in effect instigating the imperialists to threaten China with atom bombs.

[27] "The Origin and Development of the Differences between the Leadership of the CPSU and Ourselves—Comment on the Open Letter of the Central Committee of the CPSU," *Peking Review*, September 13, 1963, p. 12.

[28] See, for example, "Statement of the Soviet Government," dated August 3, 1963. Translation in *Moscow News*, reprinted in *Peking Review*, VI, No. 36 (September 6, 1963), 20. (Also reprinted from *Soviet News*, August 6, 1963, in Griffith, *The Sino-Soviet Rift*, Document 6, p. 333.)

Of course the fact that the U.S. imperialists may wish to aim more atom and hydrogen bombs at China merits attention and vigilance. But there is nothing terrifying about it. At this very moment the United States has many such bombs already poised against China. It will not make much difference if the United States listens to the Soviet leaders and adds a few more. The Chinese people will not tremble before U.S. nuclear threats. But one must ask: Where do the Soviet leaders place themselves in making such an instigation?[29]

At some time between 1958 and 1960, then, the Chinese became convinced they would not get adequate aid from the Soviet Union, and in 1960 all Soviet aid ceased. Very likely, the Chinese started to develop an independent nuclear capability in 1957–58, expecting assistance from the Soviet regime. While there may have been some delay in the original timetable, the Chinese have been able nevertheless to complete the reactors and diffusion plant started with Soviet help and may soon be able to bring their missile program to fruition.

[29] "Statement by the Spokesman of the Chinese Government—A Comment on the Soviet Government's Statement of August 21," *Peking Review*, September 6, 1963, p. 9.

4

The Detonation

On SEPTEMBER 29, 1964, ACT-
ing upon evidence of intense activity at a nuclear test site in
Central China, Secretary of State Dean Rusk issued the following statement:

> For some time it has been known that the Chinese Commu-
> nists were approaching the point where they might be able to
> detonate a first nuclear device. Such an explosion might occur
> in the near future. If it does occur, we shall know about it and
> will make the information public.
>
> It has been known since the 1950's that the Chinese Com-
> munists have been working to develop a nuclear device. They
> not only failed to sign but strongly opposed the Nuclear Test
> Ban Treaty, which has been signed by over 100 countries.
>
> The detonation of a first device does not mean a stockpile of
> nuclear weapons and the presence of modern delivery systems.
>
> The United States has fully anticipated the possibility of
> Peiping's entry into the nuclear weapons field and has taken

it into full account in determining our military posture and our own nuclear weapons program. We would deplore atmospheric testing in the face of serious efforts made by almost all other nations to protect the atmosphere from further contamination and to begin to put limitations upon a spiraling arms race.

A little more than two weeks later, on October 16, 1964, at 3:00 P.M., Peking time, the People's Republic of China exploded a uranium atomic device. The New China News Agency, eight hours later, issued a press release as follows:

> China exploded an atom bomb in the western region of China at 15:00 hours Peking Time on October 16, 1964, and thereby conducted successfully its first nuclear test.
>
> The success of China's nuclear test is a major achievement of the Chinese people in the strengthening of their national defence and safeguarding of their motherland, as well as a major contribution made by the Chinese people to the cause of the defence of world peace.
>
> The success of this test was due to the hard work and the great co-ordinated effort of China's workers, engineering and technical personnel, scientific personnel and all working personnel engaged in building up China's national defences as well as various regions and departments throughout the country who, under the leadership of the Party, displayed a spirit of relying on their own efforts and making enterprising endeavours.
>
> The Central Committee of the Chinese Communist Party and the State Council warmly congratulate them.[1]

Immediately afterwards, NCNA released a long statement by the Chinese government attempting to explain and rationalize the Chinese move. After defending China's right to produce nuclear weapons and arguing that the explosion had been carried out largely to deter American nuclear threats, the statement went on to attack the test ban treaty:

[1] Press communiqué, dated October 16, 1964. Translation in *Peking Review*, VII, No. 42 (special supplement, October 16, 1964), iii.

The Chinese government pointed out long ago that the treaty on the partial halting of nuclear tests signed by the United States, Britain and the Soviet Union in Moscow in July, 1963, was a big fraud to fool the people of the world, that it tried to consolidate the nuclear monopoly held by the three nuclear powers and tie up the hands and feet of all peace-loving countries, and that it not only did not decrease but had increased the nuclear threat of United States imperialism against the people of China and of the whole world.

The United States Government declared undisguisedly even then that the conclusion of such a treaty does not at all mean that the United States would not conduct underground tests, or would not use, manufacture, stockpile, export or proliferate nuclear weapons. The facts of the past year and more fully prove this point.

During the past year and more, the United States has not stopped manufacturing various nuclear weapons on the basis of the nuclear tests which it had already conducted. Furthermore, seeking for even greater perfection, the United States has, during this same period, conducted several dozen underground nuclear tests, and thereby perfecting the nuclear weapons it manufactures. In stationing nuclear submarines in Japan, the United States is posing a direct threat to the Japanese people, the Chinese people and the peoples of all other Asian countries.

The United States is now putting nuclear weapons into the hands of the West German revanchists through the so-called multilateral nuclear force and thereby threatens the security of the German Democratic Republic and the other East European Socialist countries.

United States submarines carrying Polaris missiles with nuclear warheads are prowling the Taiwan Strait, the Tonkin Gulf, the Mediterranean Sea, the Pacific Ocean, the Indian Ocean and the Atlantic Ocean, threatening everywhere peace-loving countries and all peoples who are fighting against imperialism, colonialism and neo-colonialism.

Under such circumstances, how can it be considered that the United States nuclear blackmail and nuclear threat against the people of the world no longer exists just because of the false impression created by the temporary halting of atmospheric tests by the United States?

The Chinese had long tended to downgrade the role of nuclear weapons in their public statements and to stress the importance of man. The "Detonation Statement" made it clear that having become a nuclear power, they were not abandoning this position:

> The atom bomb is a paper tiger. This famous saying by Chairman Mao Tse-tung is known to all. This was our view in the past and this is still our view at present. China is developing nuclear weapons not because we believe in the omnipotence of nuclear weapons and that China plans to use nuclear weapons. The truth is exactly to the contrary. In developing nuclear weapons, China's aim is to break the nuclear monopoly of the nuclear powers and to eliminate nuclear weapons.
>
> The Chinese Government is loyal to Marxism-Leninism and proletarian internationalism. We believe in the people. It is the people who decide the outcome of a war, and not any weapon. The destiny of China is decided by the Chinese people, and the destiny of the world by the peoples of the world, and not by the nuclear weapon.

The statement concluded by stressing China's desire for peace:

> The Chinese Government fully understands the good wishes of peace-loving countries and people for the halting of all nuclear tests. But more and more countries are coming to realize that the more the United States imperialists and their partners hold on to their nuclear monopoly, the more is there danger of a nuclear war breaking out.
>
> They have it and you don't, and so they are very haughty. But once those who oppose them also have it, they would no longer be so haughty, their policy of nuclear blackmail and nuclear threat would no longer be so effective, and the possibility for a complete prohibition and thorough destruction of nuclear weapons would increase. . . . Before the advent of

such a day, the Chinese Government and people will firmly and unswervingly march along their own road of strengthening their national defenses, defending their motherland and safeguarding world peace.

We are convinced that nuclear weapons, which are after all created by man, certainly will be eliminated by man.

Thus did the Chinese government not only explain its motives for acquiring nuclear weapons but also deal with some of the dangers it saw in seeking to become a nuclear power.

The American Government was clearly ready for the Chinese nuclear test. President Johnson's first remarks stressed that the test was "a tragedy for the Chinese people" because it would perpetuate their poverty; he indicated that the United States did not otherwise attach great importance to it, nor did he think it would lead to greater danger for the United States or its allies. President Johnson's statement should be quoted in full, because of its importance in setting the tone of American policy concerning the Chinese nuclear capability.

The Chinese Communists have announced that they conducted their first nuclear test today. By our own detection system we have confirmed that a low-yield test actually took place in western China at about 3 A.M. EDT.

As Secretary Rusk noted on September 29, we have known for some time that the Chinese Communists had a nuclear development program which was approaching the point of a first detonation of a test device.

This explosion comes as no surprise to the United States Government. It has been fully taken into account, in planning our own defense program and nuclear capability. Its military significance should not be overestimated. Many years and great efforts separate testing of a first nuclear device from having a stockpile of reliable weapons with effective delivery systems.

Still more basic is the fact that if and when the Chinese Communists develop nuclear weapons systems, free-world nuclear strength will continue to be enormously greater.

The United States reaffirms its defense commitments in Asia. Even if Communist China should eventually develop an effective nuclear capability, that capability would have no effect upon the readiness of the United States to respond to requests from Asian nations for help in dealing with Communist Chinese aggression. The United States will also not be diverted from its efforts to help the nations of Asia to defend themselves and to advance the welfare of their people.

The Chinese Communist nuclear weapons program is a tragedy for the Chinese people who have suffered so much under the Chinese regime. Scarce economic resources that could have been used to improve the well-being of the Chinese people have been used to produce a crude nuclear device which can only increase the sense of insecurity of the Chinese people. Other Asian nations have wisely chosen instead to work for the well-being of their people through economic development and peaceful use of the atom. In this way, they have made a great contribution to the peace and security of the world.

The Chinese Communist nuclear detonation is a reflection of policies which do not serve the cause of peace. But there is no reason to fear that it will lead to immediate dangers of war. The nations of the free world will recognize its limited significance and will persevere in their determination to preserve their independence.

We join all humanity in regretting the contamination of the atmosphere caused by the Chinese Communist test. We will continue in our efforts to keep the atmosphere clear. We will pursue with dedication and determination our purpose of achieving concrete practical steps on the road that leads away from nuclear armaments and war and toward a world of cooperation, development and peace.

The impact of this long-expected event was in a way greater than had been anticipated and in a way less. Occurring within days of the overthrow of Khrushchev in the Soviet Union, the world was still preoccupied with what was perceived to be the much more important question of what effect the change in leadership in the Kremlin would have on Soviet policy. In the

United States, which was also occupied with a presidential campaign, the Chinese nuclear detonation tended to be assessed in the light of the changes in the Kremlin and the great uncertainties for Sino-Soviet and Soviet-American relations. Similarly in India, for example, the news came on with the fear that Russia's change in leadership would alter the Soviet policy of friendship with India. Governments issued statements of one sort or another, and there was a notable stir in the press throughout the world, but within a few days the news of the Chinese bomb had been driven off the front pages. Even when it became clear that the Chinese were considerably further along in weapons development than had previously been estimated, the excitement seemed to die down quickly.

On the other hand, the Chinese test marked a significant watershed: Until it occurred, there had been some doubt, in Asia and the West, as to China's competence to achieve even those aims to which she attaches high priority and as to whether she were engaged in a substantial effort to become a nuclear power. To most Asians, the world had now changed; there are now five nuclear powers, one of them an Asian state and by virtue of that the leading power in Asia. Fear of war is combined with admiration and a feeling of satisfaction that the West's nuclear monopoly has at last been broken. At the same time, it is clear—to whatever extent the United States sought to and actually did downgrade the importance of the initial test—notwithstanding that the world must now begin to deal with a China that will soon be capable of wreaking great destruction, at least on her neighbors. The pressure to accept her as a world power and specifically to permit her entrance into the United Nations has substantially increased. The view that the United States is hiding her head in the sand by refusing to recognize Communist China has become even more difficult to oppose.

Thus, the Chinese leaders undoubtedly look with considerable satisfaction on their achievement in carrying out the nuclear test despite the Soviet Union's withdrawal of support in 1960 and active opposition ever since. They undoubtedly look upon October 16, 1964, as a milestone on China's road to world power and eventual triumph over the United States.

Nevertheless, the detonation of a nuclear device was not without costs and dangers to Peking, and the Chinese leaders were aware of this. In the "Detonation Statement" itself, they made it clear that China was sensitive to and was trying to deal with at least two of the problems: the widespread world opposition to further testing of nuclear weapons; and the fear that the United States (or perhaps the Soviet Union) might use the event as an excuse to launch an attack against China (perhaps restricted to Chinese nuclear facilities).

In dealing with the first problem, the Chinese statement fell back on essentially the same position the Chinese had adopted toward the test ban treaty:

> The Chinese Government has consistently advocated the complete prohibition and thorough destruction of nuclear weapons. Should this have been realized, China need not have developed the nuclear weapon. But this position of ours has met the stubborn resistance of the United States imperialists.
>
> The Chinese Government pointed out long ago that the treaty on the partial halting of nuclear tests signed by the United States, Britain and the Soviet Union in Moscow in July, 1963, was a big fraud to fool the people of the world. . . .
>
> The Chinese Government hereby formally proposes to the governments of the world that a summit conference of all the countries of the world be convened to discuss the question of the complete prohibition and thorough destruction of nuclear weapons, and that, as a first step, the summit conference should reach an agreement to the effect that the nuclear powers and those countries which will soon become nuclear powers undertake not to use nuclear weapons, neither to use them against non-nuclear countries and nuclear-free zones, nor against each other.

If those countries in possession of huge quantities of nuclear weapons are not even willing to undertake not to use them, how can those countries not yet in possession of them be expected to believe in their sincerity for peace and not to adopt possible and necessary defensive measures?

The Chinese Government will, as always, exert every effort to promote the realization of the noble aim of the complete prohibition and thorough destruction of nuclear weapons through international consultations. . . .

We are convinced that nuclear weapons, which are after all created by man, certainly will be eliminated by man.

As with the test ban treaty, the Chinese followed up the statement calling for total nuclear disarmament with a letter to all the heads of government. Sent on October 17, over the signature of Premier Chou En-lai, it read as follows:

On October 16, 1964, China exploded an atom bomb, thus successfully making its first nuclear test. On the same day, the Chinese Government issued a statement on this event, setting forth in detail China's position on the question of nuclear weapons.

The Chinese Government consistently stands for the complete prohibition and thorough destruction of nuclear weapons. China has been compelled to conduct nuclear testing and develop nuclear weapons. China's mastering of nuclear weapons is entirely for defence and for protecting the Chinese people from the U.S. nuclear threat.

The Chinese Government solemnly declares that at no time and in no circumstances will China be the first to use nuclear weapons.

The Chinese Government will continue to work for the complete prohibition and thorough destruction of nuclear weapons through international consultations and, for this purpose, has put forward in its statement the following proposal:

That a summit conference of all the countries of the world be convened to discuss the question of the complete prohibition and thorough destruction of nuclear weapons, and that as the first step, the summit conference should reach an agreement to the effect that the nuclear powers and those countries which may soon become nuclear powers undertake not to use nuclear weapons, neither to use them against non-nuclear countries and nuclear-free zones, nor against each other.

It is the common aspiration of all peace-loving countries and people of the world to prevent a nuclear war and eliminate nuclear weapons. The Chinese Government sincerely hopes that its proposal will be given favourable consideration and positive response by your Government.[2]

The Chinese Communist government made use of the informal contact it maintains in Poland with the United States Ambassador there to send this letter to Washington. This was the first time that an official Chinese statement had been sent to the United States through the Sino-American ambassadorial link. While the British Government announced that it was "studying" the Chinese proposal, American officials rejected it, terming it a "smoke screen."[3]

After the test ban treaty was signed, the Chinese had been made clearly aware of the unpopularity of their position. During his trip to Africa in 1964, for example, Chou En-lai had been asked repeatedly to explain the Chinese opposition to the treaty, and he had done so by quoting the Chinese post-test-ban statements.[4] In order to fend off similar criticism following their explosion of a bomb, the Chinese launched a counter-offensive in the disarmament field which had considerable success. First, they detailed again their objections to the test ban treaty and why they thought it a fraud designed to perpetuate the nuclear monopoly of the super-powers. They went on from there, however, to take the offensive by stressing

2 "Premier Chou Cables Government Heads of the World," *Peking Review*, October 23, 1964, p. 6.
3 *The New York Times*, October 22, 1964, p. 3.
4 See Robert A. Scalapino, "Sino-Soviet Competition in Africa," *Foreign Affairs*, XLII (July, 1964), 643.

their positive interest in arms-control agreements. They not only reiterated their earlier proposals for a nuclear-weapon–free zone in the Pacific and for total destruction of atomic weapons, but also called for an agreement among the nuclear powers not to use atomic weapons—in fact making a unilateral declaration that China would never be the first to use nuclear weapons. At the same time, they pointed to a major vulnerability in the American position by indicating that the United States had in the past refused to make such a statement and in fact has emphasized her right to use nuclear weapons first in the event of an aggression that it felt could not be contained by any other means. Thus, in a sense, the Chinese were able to make the situation symmetrical: While the United States signs the test ban treaty and calls upon China to do likewise as a prerequisite for further steps in disarmament, the Chinese commit themselves to a nuclear-weapons policy that rules out a first strike and calls upon the United States to accept this position before moving on to other agreements. Moreover, the Chinese maintained, they had specifically proposed a whole series of agreements leading to total nuclear disarmament, while the United States argued that total nuclear disarmament was impossible because hidden stocks of nuclear material could never be fully eradicated. This line of reasoning was made explicit in a *People's Daily* editorial:

This concrete proposal by the Chinese Government that an agreement be reached first on not using nuclear weapons is practical, fair and reasonable, easily feasible and involves no question of control. If all the countries concerned are willing to make this commitment, then the danger of nuclear war will be immediately reduced. And this would mean a big initial step towards the ultimate goal of complete prohibition and thorough destruction of nuclear weapons. After that, it would be possible to discuss the questions of the halting of all kinds of nuclear tests, the prohibition of the export, import, proliferation, manufacture, stockpiling and destruction of nuclear weapons. Obviously, the U.S. Government has no reason at all to reject this proposal if it has the slightest desire for peace.

Johnson, however, avoided making any reference to the Chinese Government's proposal in his statement and television speech. Instead, he talked profusely about the need for China to accede to the tripartite partial nuclear test ban treaty, for the conclusion of a verified agreement on the ending of all kinds of nuclear tests, for efforts to prevent nuclear proliferation and for the non-nuclear countries to accept the protection of the U.S. "nuclear umbrella." To borrow a word Rusk used to attack China, Johnson's pack of proposals is simply a "smoke-screen" to conceal the obstinate and feeble stand of the United States which dares not undertake that it will not be the first to use nuclear weapons.[5]

By stressing their commitment to peace and desire for nuclear disarmament, the Chinese have been fairly successful in reducing the immediate adverse reaction to their first nuclear test. Cambodia, Indonesia, and several African states—in addition to China's Communist allies—welcomed the test as a step toward world peace; few countries were willing to condemn it outright. Despite their opposition to the Chinese effort to become a nuclear power, most Afro-Asian nations simply expressed their regret that a nuclear test was necessary and stressed the importance of bringing China into the United Nations and into disarmament talks. The Secretary-General of the United Nations, U Thant, in fact proposed a conference of the five nuclear powers on the question of nuclear disarmament,[6] and, if, as it appears at least possible, China is admitted to the U.N. in 1965, it will be in part because of her nuclear test. The failure of India's Prime Minister, Lal Bahadur Shastri, to gain support for the proposal made at the Cairo Conference in October, 1964, to send a delegation to Peking to urge China not to test nuclear weapons, underlines

5 Reprinted in *Peking Review,* VII, No. 44 (October 30, 1964), 6–7.
6 *The New York Times,* October 23, 1964, p. 1.

the caution with which most countries treat the emergence of a nuclear China.

In addition to nations allied with the United States, only India and Japan condemned the Chinese nuclear test immediately after the detonation. These two both decried the test as a threat to world peace requiring them to re-examine their own military programs; in both cases, however, the governments reaffirmed that their countries would not become nuclear powers. The most immediate adverse reaction to the Chinese detonation was in Japan, where even the left wing of the Japanese Socialist Party, which is generally pro-Chinese, condemned it; a delegation of the Socialist Party visiting in Peking even spoke out against the test at a public banquet, when their hosts made favorable references to China's effort to become a nuclear power.[7] The Socialist Party is expected therefore to move further from the policy of *rapprochement* with China, just as the Japanese Communist Party is expected to be further isolated from other left-wing groups by its support of the test.

The Chinese promise never to be the first to use nuclear weapons is a theme that runs through all the efforts to counteract the adverse reaction to the Chinese position on nuclear testing and through the articulation of their policy of not provoking an American attack on China.[8] For the Chinese leaders are aware that China's testing of a nuclear device—her attempt to become a nuclear power—brings closer the possibility that the United States (or perhaps the Soviet Union) will decide to destroy the Chinese capability to produce nuclear weapons before China has an effective deterrent against such a move. In order to keep this from happening, China can be expected to be even more cautious in taking military action around her periphery than she has been in the past, at least until she has

[7] *Ibid.*, October 18, 1964, p. 41.

[8] On whether the United States should in fact attack the Chinese nuclear installations, see Chapter 5.

a nuclear-weapons delivery system. At the same time, she will probably continue to proclaim not only that she will not be the first to use nuclear weapons but also that she understands the grave consequences of nuclear war, that she will not, therefore, aggressively threaten the use of nuclear weapons, and that she will strive to prevent nuclear war. All these themes were touched on in the Chinese "Detonation Statement":

> On the question of nuclear weapons, China will commit neither the error of adventurism nor the error of capitulationism. The Chinese people can be trusted. . . . We sincerely hope that a nuclear war would never occur. We are convinced that, so long as all peace-loving countries and people of the world make common efforts and persist in the struggle, a nuclear war can be prevented.

Thus, for the next few years, until China acquires a militarily useful nuclear capability, there will probably be a hiatus in major foreign-policy ventures on her part, providing an opportunity for the United States to deal with the problems created by her detonation of a nuclear bomb and those that will arise when Chinese nuclear weapons threaten her Asian neighbors.

5

Guidelines for American Policy

T HE STEPS THE UNITED STATES
should take to deal with a nuclear armed China must fit into
and be part of the total American policy in the Far East. The
explosion of a nuclear device by the Chinese has, as could
have been predicted, forced a careful re-evaluation of just
what United States interests are in the Far East, what areas
she is prepared to defend, and in what ways she should be
prepared to defend them. This political evaluation should
have been carried out prior to the detonation, rather than in
reaction to it. A Chinese nuclear capability need not be a
major determinant of American policy in, for example, Laos,
Vietnam, or India, but should nevertheless be a factor influ-
encing American policy, and the sooner it is taken fully into
account the better.

97

If for whatever reason there is to be any retrenchment in American commitments in the Far East, it is vital that it not appear to come in reaction to the Chinese detonation or to a modest Chinese nuclear capability. For example, an American withdrawal from Vietnam would have grave consequences in any case, but the consequences of a withdrawal if it appeared to be the result of the detonation, as it inevitably would now, would be far more grave. Such a withdrawal would undermine the American argument that Chinese nuclear demonstrations cannot in any way affect the nuclear military balance in Asia for a long time to come. The American withdrawal of some forces from Japan in December, 1963, had much less serious consequences than it would have had if carried out after the Chinese nuclear detonation.

In considering an American policy to anticipate an effective Chinese nuclear capability, one must ask: First, what kind of military and political posture the United States should maintain; second, what information should the United States convey to Asian countries; and, third, what kind of message does the United States wish to convey to the Peking regime about its likely reaction to a developing Chinese nuclear program. The favorable opportunities created by a Chinese nuclear capability for effective relations with some groups in Japan should be considered, for example, along with the threat it will pose. American public and private attitudes toward Sino-Soviet relations must also be taken into account, as well as possibilities for Soviet-American cooperation in dealing with a nuclear China.

THE AMERICAN MILITARY POSTURE

Any Chinese nuclear capability of the foreseeable future is unlikely to pose a direct military threat to the continental United States. Nevertheless, it needs to be asked whether any change in the American military posture in the Pacific should be made in order to deal with Chinese threats: On the one hand, what actual military measures are necessary; on the other, what kind of public statements might or should be made about these measures?

The United States currently has a large and powerful nuclear force around the borders of Communist China. In addition to the forces of the Seventh Fleet, the United States has nuclear-armed planes as well as short-range rockets stationed in various places in Asia. One Polaris submarine armed with missiles capable of reaching any important military target on the Chinese mainland is already cruising in the Pacific, and additional submarines can be shifted to the Pacific on very short notice. Finally, the American intercontinental striking force of Strategic Air Command (SAC) bombers and ICBM's can be targeted against Chinese military and industrial targets, as well as those in the Soviet Union. In March, 1964, the United States moved fifteen B-52 bombers to Guam, replacing a squadron of older B-47 bombers. When and if heavy bombers are phased out in the 1970's, the TFX fighter bomber will be capable of launching nuclear strikes against China; it has, indeed, apparently been designed in part for this mission.[1] In addition, American ground and air forces are equipped with a variety of tactical nuclear weapons capable of being used against Chinese forces engaged in offensive operations or against limited military targets within China.

There does not appear to be any need to augment the nuclear capability of the United States in the Pacific theater within the next five years, beyond the already scheduled assignment of additional Polaris submarines to the area as they become available. (In modernizing existing weapon systems, however, attention should be given to the possible vulner-

---

[1] U.S. Senate Committee on Armed Services, 88th Cong., 2nd sess., *Hearings on Fiscal Year 1965* (Washington, D.C.: U.S. Government Printing Office, 1964), p. 65.

ability of current weapons to a primitive Chinese nuclear attack.) American nuclear strength in the Pacific is more than sufficient to deter any Chinese use of nuclear weapons and should also be sufficient to give credence to any threat the United States might want to make to counter a Chinese nuclear offensive.

Nevertheless, there remains the question of the declared policy to accompany this American nuclear force. It is clear that problems are raised in many countries by proposals to establish bases and to station nuclear weapons. American forces in Japan, for example, are not equipped with nuclear weapons for this reason. However, other American allies, in particular South Korea and Taiwan, are not unwilling to let nuclear weapons be placed on their territory, and the United States has its own forces in Okinawa, at Clark Air Force Base in the Philippines, at Pearl Harbor, and on the ships of the Seventh Fleet. Public stress on American nuclear capability will incur some criticism, however, in particular in Japan, and at the same time could counteract the American policy of minimizing the importance of nuclear weapons. Nevertheless, on balance, it would seem desirable for the United States to give greater publicity to her existing nuclear force in the Pacific theater—not in a dramatic way, but in a series of calm announcements and moves demonstrating that the United States has maintained and will continue to maintain substantial nuclear forces to deal with any Soviet or Chinese aggressive military move in the Far East. A step in this direction was taken in October, 1964, after the detonation of the Chinese bomb, when the Pentagon announced that it had moved B-52's to Guam during the previous March.[2] At the same time, it might be well for the United States to make clearer what should already be abundantly clear—it certainly is to American military policy-makers—that American forces based in the Pacific and in the United States can be used

[2] *The New York Times,* October 27, 1964, p. 6.

against China without triggering the entire strategic force. Contingency plans should be carefully drawn up, if they do not already exist, to enable the United States to mount an attack on Chinese forces all the way from the use of a single tactical nuclear weapon to a large-scale strike designed to destroy the military and industrial centers of China without using forces that are considered necessary to deter the Soviet Union and without triggering the Soviet force. For the United States to create a separate Pacific nuclear force might be going too far in this direction and give more weight to China's nuclear threat than it deserves. The United States need merely indicate that she has forces in the Pacific which she can use without launching her strategic forces against her major opponent, the Soviet Union. It should be clear to American military planners that contingencies requiring this capability may arise, and the command structures and forces for carrying them out should be available.

American conventional strength will, of course, continue to be at least as important in the Pacific theater as American nuclear strength, for the governments and people of that area have a vital concern in the question of whether the United States is prepared to use conventional forces to cope with low-level Chinese military threats and with Chinese aid to indigenous Communist forces. American policy-makers must bear in mind that the Chinese threat, as assessed by most Asians, remains one of political subversion, guerrilla warfare, and conventional military attacks. The explosion of a nuclear device by China mainly served to remind them of the presence of a major military power on their borders, but they continue to see that power largely if not wholly in conventional military terms. It is thus important for the United States to make it clear that indigenous forces, complemented by American conventional strength, are capable of containing any Chinese aggression and that this strength will be employed when and if necessary. At the present time, the United States has a sizable force in South Vietnam; it has two divisions in Korea, to augment the South Korean forces against the possible renewal of aggression by North Korea aided by China; in addition, there are ground forces scattered throughout the area, in particular in Hawaii, and a Marine division scattered in Okinawa, Hawaii, and with the fleet. These forces appear to be if anything too small to impress the Asians as able to cope adequately with Chinese forces in a conventional war beyond China's borders. Besides making the presence of these forces felt among allies and neutrals, therefore, the United States should call attention to the growing strength of the continental Strike Command, with its ready combat divisions and extensive airlift and sealift capabilities. In addition, the possibility of providing a well-publicized seaborne stockpile of material for several divisions in Asia—corresponding to such stockpiling in Europe—should be considered, in order to emphasize the United States' willingness to commit forces where necessary and her ability to do so rapidly and effectively. The United States has already stockpiled some material on ships anchored in the Philippines, and an airlift exercise was conducted in early 1964.[3]

The United States also needs to consider the question of when and how she might want to initiate the use of tactical nuclear weapons. The Sino-Soviet dispute increases the improbability of Soviet interferences should the United States make limited use of tactical nuclear weapons in retaliation for Chinese aggression or even, perhaps, should the United States launch a major nuclear attack against the Chinese mainland. But though the United States may well want to act as if she believes that the Soviet Union would not interfere in a Sino-American war, Russian acquiescence is hardly the only consideration in deciding whether to use tactical nuclear weapons to defend Asian countries against overt Chinese aggression.

[3] *Ibid.,* January 14, 1964, p. 2; January 31, 1964, p. 9.

There is no doubt that the use of tactical nuclear weapons against an opponent with a small nuclear capability produces a military advantage. But will the Chinese ever mount a conventional military attack of the kind that can be affected by the use of tactical nuclear weapons? The Chinese are unlikely to provide the United States with a situation in which the American use of nuclear weapons could be politically defensible or even militarily desirable. All along her borders—in India and in the Taiwan Straits—China has been willing to use military force and to aid indigenous Communist forces, but she has always done so (at least since 1950) in ways that failed to present either a clear-cut case of all-out overt aggression or a situation in which the use of nuclear weapons was urgent or advisable. Since there is nothing to suggest that she will abandon this mode of conduct, the military challenges she poses will require that the United States be able to give military aid for counter-subversive warfare and to place American manpower in the field where it seems necessary to do so.

It is extremely unlikely that the Soviet Union will decide categorically to tolerate any use of atomic arms against China regardless of circumstances; and it is even less likely that she will reveal her plans. Therefore, despite the degree to which the Sino-Soviet relationship deteriorates, the United States Government must weigh the possibility that use of nuclear weapons against Chinese troops (or in fact any troops) would force the Soviet Union to enter the war or at least supply nuclear weapons to China. Soviet intervention would make the securing of American objectives more difficult, could result in irresistible pressures to make concessions outside Asia or to an explosion into a Soviet-American nuclear war. These fearful possibilities can never and should never be forgotten when considering either the employment of nuclear weapons or any other military or political move throughout the world. On these grounds alone, it is doubtful whether

American military commanders will ever be given the authority to launch tactical nuclear weapons against China. This is not to say that there may not be occasions on which it would make military sense to do so, but only to suggest that the fear of general nuclear war alone may continue to be sufficient to deter such a political decision no matter what the state of Sino-Soviet relations.

In addition, however, the possible political consequences of using tactical nuclear weapons continues to be serious. The aversion to nuclear weapons felt in most Asian countries has been evident in their favorable reaction to the nuclear test ban treaty and in motions for which they have pressed in the U.N. General Assembly calling for nuclear free zones, bans on the use of nuclear weapons, and the like. Any use of nuclear weapons by the United States in Asia would have serious political drawbacks. Moreover, to use nuclear weapons once in local warfare makes it more likely that they will be used again: The tacit ban against them that has done much to prevent the outbreak of large-scale wars in the postwar period would have been breached. Once a nuclear weapon is used in war, it would be difficult to return to the situation in which there is a general expectation that nuclear weapons will not be used and that, when they are used, the world is close to all-out war.[4] Finally, the country in whose defense the United States proposes to use nuclear weapons might veto their use—for political reasons or out of fear of the destruction that would result.

It is unlikely that the United States will be in a situation in which the winning of a single battle seems to outweigh the political disadvantages that will always accompany the use of tactical nuclear weapons. There are reasons for the United States to build up a tactical nuclear capability in the Pacific

[4] See Thomas C. Schelling, "Nuclear Weapons and Limited War," in *The Strategy of Conflict* (Cambridge, Mass.: Harvard University Press, 1960), pp. 257–66.

—not simply to win single battles but to stem the tide, for example, of a large-scale Chinese invasion of India. The United States should indicate, however, that she can deal with low levels of Chinese aggression with her own and allied conventional forces. Large-scale military threats, such as an invasion of India or Taiwan, might be met not with the tactical use of nuclear weapons on the battlefield but rather with the use of strategic nuclear weapons designed to destroy China's warmaking capability.

Tactical nuclear weapons have an important deterrent effect, but to see them as a substitute for conventional military power is to misunderstand the political significance of a large American military presence in the Far East. Their value as a substitute is also questionable in view of the fact that in a moment of crisis the American President is unlikely to authorize their use.

American Policy Toward Allies and Neutrals

It can never be overemphasized that the development of a modest Chinese nuclear capability should be only one factor, and a relatively minor one, in determining what American policy should be in relation to the countries bordering China or on such issues as the future role of the Southeast Asia Treaty Organization or American-Indian relations. We are concerned here with the specific problem of what actions the United States should take in relation to the nations of Asia in order to anticipate a militarily effective Chinese nuclear capability.

The United States will want to continue to stress the great difficulty and expense involved in developing a nuclear capability, as well as the period that must elapse before China will have a usable nuclear force, so as to put any Chinese nuclear detonation in its proper perspective. It might also serve to deter other countries from embarking on national nuclear programs, if they understood the sacrifices such programs entail in terms of internal economic development and standard of living. The sophistication the United States can expect about the development of nuclear capabilities will vary from country to country and from group to group, but the difficulties and costs of a nuclear program are so overwhelming as to be widely understood in Asia.

United States efforts to convince the Asian nations that it is not necessary to have nuclear weapons involves both political prestige and military security. In contrasting the present situation in the Far East with those of the past in Europe, it is important to realize that the main political problems frustrating the American effort to halt the spread of nuclear weapons in Europe are not likely to exist in the Far East: In her relations with Britain, France, and Germany, the United States is dealing with great powers who, in giving up the effort to obtain national nuclear forces, would in effect be giving up their present and future claim to world-power status, whether as independent nations or united in a federated Europe. It is this political factor, and the desire for increased status in political negotiations, that has been at the back of the drives for national and international nuclear forces in Europe. In Asia, the United States is dealing with very different countries, which, with the exception of Japan and China, have never aspired to world-power status. In choosing not to produce nuclear weapons, these countries will be following their traditional course of maintaining a military capability less powerful than other nations' and relying upon allies for their security. The prestige, or lack of it, accorded to nuclear power will also be an important part of the evolving Asian attitudes toward nuclear weapons. Whereas nuclear weapons have some appeal to certain politically significant groups in Europe, they have none for most of the powerful political groups in India, Japan, and elsewhere in the Far East. The generally left-wing and to some extent pacifist orientation of most political groups in the Asian countries makes them to some extent uninterested in the achievement of national nuclear power and uneasy about the acquisition of nuclear weapons from an ally.

Furthermore, it should be noted that the French experience has persuaded many political leaders in Asia of the wisdom of not trying to acquire nuclear weapons. It seems to many Asian groups that France gained little political prestige or influence from her acquisition of nuclear weapons—an impression the United States, the Soviet Union, and other countries have helped to foster by deriding the French accomplishment and arguing that it has not at all enhanced France's status as a political power in the world. Thus the French experience has been useful not only in emphasizing the great cost and difficulty involved in developing an independent nuclear program, but also in showing that the political gains from a nuclear program are not necessarily great and in fact may not exist at all.

All this could change, of course; the situation already became less favorable to halting the spread of nuclear weapons with the Chinese detonation of a device. If, on the one hand, China's acquisition of nuclear weapons enhances her standing in the international arena to the degree that she is called the only important power in the Far East, then other countries feel it necessary to acquire nuclear weapons; on the other hand, the general world-wide trend in the development of nuclear weapons affects their political acceptability in the largest states of Asia—if, for example, proliferation reaches countries in the Middle East, Asian nations may decide they need nuclear weapons merely to retain a place as secondary powers.

While the political incentives to acquire nuclear weapons are likely to be fewer in Asia than in Europe, the security motives may be stronger. The United States' attachment to and commitment to defend Europe is clearly greater than her commitment to any nation in Asia and will remain so no matter what declarations are made by the United States. Certainly the Asian powers recognize this—that a commitment to wage war to protect not only Western Europe but also the isolated city of Berlin is not likely to be accorded to any nation in the Far East. In considering their long-run security prospects, the Asian nations are more likely than the European powers to question the ability and willingness of the United States to come to their aid.

Since most of these countries fear China more than the Soviet Union, they will also be influenced by knowledge that for the indefinite future the Chinese will have a much smaller nuclear capability than the Soviet Union. This has two implications. It means that these countries can match Communist China in nuclear strength if they so desire; India, Japan, and eventually other states could have nuclear forces equal to those of the Chinese if they were prepared to commit large portions of their Gross National Product to acquire them. Unlike the French, for example, who can at best hope only to have a force capable of destroying a few Soviet cities, the major powers of Asia could match the Chinese threat if they decided it was worth doing so. But it also means that the Chinese force will not pose a significant threat to the United States. The major security issue that has made it difficult for the United States to halt the spread of nuclear weapons in Europe has been the argument that she would no longer be prepared to defend Europe when the Soviet Union could threaten large-scale damage to the United States. This argument, already dubious for Europe, will not even be applicable to China for some time. Assuming possible developments in defensive weapons systems, including anti-missile missiles, one could hypothesize that for an indefinite period, China will be unable to deliver a significant number of nuclear weapons against American territory. Therefore, while the American political commitment to nations of the Far East is significantly less than her commitment to Europe, the risks for the United States of using nuclear weapons in defense of Asian powers may also be less than the risks in their use against the Soviet Union in defense of Europe.

The nations of Asia will not rule out the possibility of obtaining help from the Soviet Union in the event of aggression—especially nuclear aggression—by China. The Soviet Union is at the present time supplying conventional military aid to India. She has supplied Indonesia as well as India with weapons more modern than those she gave the Chinese. Thus it is not unreasonable for Asian countries to believe that they may be able to count, in some circumstances, on Soviet as well as American nuclear aid in the event of Chinese nuclear aggression. The Soviet Union is also likely to put pressure on the Chinese to prevent their using nuclear weapons.

In addition to convincing the countries of Asia that it is not in their interest to produce nuclear weapons, the United States must assure them that she is able and willing to help them defend their independence against subversion or overt conventional aggression and, especially, persuade them of her readiness to respond to any Chinese Communist use of nuclear weapons with a counter-use of nuclear weapons. The United States will not want to stand by and permit the Chinese to use nuclear weapons without nuclear retaliation, and there is no reason not to be absolutely clear about this.[5] This was clearly in President Johnson's mind when, two days after the detonation of China's bomb, he declared:

Communist China's expensive and demanding effort tempts other states to equal folly. Nuclear spread is dangerous to all mankind.

[5] Such a pledge would raise the danger that a nation might seek to provoke China to use nuclear weapons in order to bring on an American response. The nation concerned, however, would be risking major nuclear damage to its territory, and it is likely to be difficult to provoke the Chinese to use nuclear weapons.

What if there should come to be ten nuclear powers, or twenty?

What if we must learn to look everywhere for the restraint which our own example now sets for a few? Will the human race be safe in such a day?

The lesson of Lop Nor is that we are right to recognize the danger of nuclear spread. We must continue to work against it—and we will.

First, we will continue to support the limited test ban treaty, which has made the air cleaner. We call on the world—especially Red China—to join the nations which have signed it.

Second, we will continue to work for an ending of all nuclear tests of every kind, by solid and verified agreement.

Third, we continue to believe that the struggle against nuclear spread is as much in the Soviet interest as in our own. We will be ready to join with them and all the world—in working to avoid it.

Fourth, the nations that do not seek national nuclear weapons can be sure that if they need our strong support against some threat of blackmail, they will have it.[6]

The difficulty of developing a nuclear capability and the difference between a mere nuclear device and an effective military delivery system have already been understood in Asia. Perhaps the greatest sophistication on this score is to be found in Japan. Among all but a few knowledgeable Japanese, there seems to be a general consensus on the undesirability of a Japanese national nuclear program, and a clear understanding of the problems China will face in seeking to develop her national nuclear force and which Japan would also face if she followed suit. Both among the left-wing political groups and in the right-wing ruling conservative party, as well as in journalistic and academic circles, there is considerable familiarity with these problems. The possibility of a Chinese nuclear device being detonated had been under active discussion in Japan for several years prior to the actual event, and

[6] Speech of October 18, 1964.

the dominant theme of those discussions was precisely this distinction between a mere detonation and a serious military capability that could threaten Japan or other nations in the Far East. This is not to say that the Japanese do not appreciate the political significance—in other countries as well as in Japan—of a Chinese nuclear capability. At the level of conscious awareness of the technical realities of nuclear production, however, there is little need for American educational efforts. The immediate Japanese reaction to the test ban treaty was a reassertion of the limited nature of the added threat and the continuing undesirability of a Japanese nuclear program. It may be desirable for the Japanese to undertake more extensive education of the general population about these problems, but this can best be handled by the Japanese themselves, with discreet American assistance if need be.

In India, as well, there is comprehension of the realities of nuclear-weapons production. That in a technological sense a nuclear option is open to India is recognized, but, at least before the Chinese detonation of a device, it looked unattractive politically and economically. Both before and after India's border flare-ups with China, the late Prime Minister Nehru—in press conferences, statements, political speeches, and debates in Parliament—displayed his understanding of the problems of developing a nuclear capability, and of the long road China must travel before she has such a capability. Indeed, Nehru's statement at a press conference on December 31, 1962, expresses well the message the United States seeks to convey to Asian nations:

> *Prime Minister:* . . . About China having nuclear bombs, it is quite possible that in a year's time or two years, they might have a nuclear test. I do not think they will ever have any nuclear force worth the name to offer, I mean at any foreseeable time.
> *Question:* Are they capable of doing it, Sir?
> *Prime Minister:* Not scientifically, but a nuclear test does not

mean that a person who has got it is capable of making nuclear warfare. One test, suppose they have it, will have a psychological effect, and some weak-kneed people in India might have their knees wobbling and develop cold feet. It will not have the slightest effect on India as such, if they have a test tomorrow. They will have to have numerous tests year after year, and then comes the time to build up the thing, which takes years, a number of years. Even if they have the test, they cannot be ready to use it. Of course, it will have a psychological effect, I admit it. If I may say so, take even a great country like France, which has got some nuclear bombs, but nothing much even that [sic].

Why I say China is not likely to have it, is because in the present stage of China's industrial development, they can, with great effort, if [China] pours in enough funds and some scientific material, do it. I have no doubt that they have got some scientists good enough for it, but the resources necessary for this kind of thing are very great. It is one thing to have some nuclear tests, but quite another thing to build up some nuclear bombs, or whatever they are called, for use. I still maintain what I said previously that although we are not going to make bombs, not even thinking of making bombs, we are in nuclear science more advanced than China.[7]

A year later, in what was described by Indian officials as the inauguration of a new policy of stimulating discussion of nuclear affairs in India, Nehru asserted that a Chinese nuclear explosion need not frighten India because "it is a long way" from an experimental bomb to a military capability.[8] Following China's detonation of a bomb, however, the climate in India began to change so as to suggest that India might well decide to launch her own nuclear-weapons program. Prime Minister Lal Bahadur Shastri, while acknowledging the pressure to change India's policy, reiterated that India would not seek to manufacture nuclear weapons. The ruling Congress

7 Government of India, Prime Minister's press conference, December 31, 1962 (mimeographed). See also *The Washington Post*, January 1, 1963.
8 *The New York Times*, October 3, 1963, p. 9.

Party, after some debate, affirmed this decision, but others began to question whether India could maintain the policy. Dr. Homi J. Bhabha, Director of the Indian Atomic Energy Agency, warned that India might be forced to make nuclear weapons "unless some important and tangible steps are taken towards general disarmament." He estimated that India could produce a ten-kiloton bomb within eighteen months at a cost of $368,000.[9]

But the nuclear facts of life are more widely known in Japan and India than in other nations of Asia; the education of governments and élite groups as to the limited importance of the Chinese detonation of a bomb should be continued, particularly in the nations where it has not progressed as far. It is important that this education be accurate, neither underestimating nor overestimating the importance of a Chinese nuclear capability. As for the assessment of the actual military force the Chinese may develop, the states of Asia would do well to realize that within five years this will include some deliverable weapons, and that such weapons may pose military threats that will have to be dealt with in collaboration with the United States. Governments should be made aware, if they are not already, that there is a vast difference between intellectually understanding China's nuclear detonation and emotionally reacting to it, not only among the people but also among members of government.

In attempting to reach political understandings with the nations of Asia, it is important to bear in mind the extreme volatility of the situation: New rulers will take office; governments may drastically shift their orientation—as in India when China attacked her border, or as might occur in Indonesia if a pro-Communist government or pro-Western military regime were to replace Sukarno. In Japan, there is the possibility of a socialist regime; discussion of political issues of this kind would be very different with it than with the conservative

[9] *Ibid.*, October 27, 1964, p. 5.

government, for the Socialists might well have abandoned opposition to the Japanese-American security pact before coming to power but might still want friendlier relations with Communist China and might still oppose an increased Japanese defense effort.

The United States Government should take care to avoid the mistake it made in Europe of stressing the value of nuclear weapons for defense. When the United States Government made the decision to do this in the early years of the Eisenhower Administration, it did so while facing a Soviet Union with a nuclear capability considerably less developed than that of the United States, particularly at the tactical level. At that time, the United States convinced her European allies that nuclear weapons would serve as a substitute for manpower and would be an effective deterrent and defense against Soviet conventional forces. In arguing for this policy, the United States not only vitiated the pressures to create adequate conventional forces in Europe, but also added to the prestige of nuclear weapons so as later to make it hard to halt their spread in Europe. These mistakes have not yet been made in Asia, and, though the European experience has had some impact, it is still not too late to instill among the Asian elite a different image of the role of nuclear weapons. The United States should persuade the governments of Asia that their political prestige will not be significantly increased by the development of a nuclear capability and that, in fact, her willingness to be involved in their defense may decline if they develop nuclear weapons and hence are able to bring her into a nuclear war. Here, the American attitude toward the French and British nuclear programs in the last several years might be discreetly alluded to, to underline these points.

The United States may also want to raise the question of concrete defense measures against Chinese weapons. A genuine Chinese nuclear capability is certainly several years away, but the governments may want now, rather than later, to decide to allow American forces on their territory.

The smaller nations of Asia that have no means of developing their own nuclear capability pose no obstacles to acceptance of the American policy of opposing the spread of nuclear weapons, but there is the possibility that they will accept Chinese hegemony. To prevent this, the United States needs to employ conventional forces and to provide political and economic assistance, but she must also assure these countries that the existence of a Chinese nuclear capability has not seriously affected the military balance in the Far East or reduced American willingness to come to their aid. They must be convinced that a Chinese nuclear capability makes U.S. intervention more rather than less likely.

THE ROLE OF ARMS CONTROL

In most discussions of a test ban before the treaty was signed and in the evaluations of it that followed, attention was focused primarily on the effects of a test ban on the Soviet-American nuclear balance of power.[10] But the major effects of the test ban are likely to be in the Far East. The predictions of most analysts that China would refuse to sign a test ban treaty have turned out to be correct. Nevertheless, these analysts failed to observe the important political consequences of the test ban vis-à-vis the impact of China's detonation of a bomb and her ultimate nuclear capability.

Almost every country in the world except China and France now consider nuclear tests to be illegal. All the non-Communist Asian countries except Cambodia signed the test ban treaty. When China detonated an atomic device, then, she was, in the eyes of these countries, violating an international agreement that was subscribed to by most of the nations of the world. Rather than engaging in an activity that was also being carried by other major powers, China was demonstrat-

[10] See, for example, U.S. Senate, 88th Cong., 1st sess., Committee on Foreign Relations, *Hearings, Nuclear Test Ban Treaty*, August 12–15, 19–23, 26–27, 1963 (Washington, D.C.: U.S. Government Printing Office, 1963). Hereafter cited as *Senate Test Ban Hearings*.

ing her disdain for international opinion. The test ban treaty made it politically more difficult and costly for left-wing groups in nations like Japan, which had previously been friendly to China, to continue to defend her policies. As the Chinese must recognize, the political advantages they hoped to gain from nuclear testing were reduced by the treaty.

The test ban treaty also seriously affected the likely future course of any nuclear proliferation in the Far East. The fact that India, Japan, and other Asian countries signed the test ban treaty makes it more difficult to alter their decision not to become nuclear powers and less likely that they will do so. For the embarrassment of violating an international agreement—although the option to do so is provided in the clause giving the right of withdrawal in the event of exceptional circumstances—will make it even more difficult than it would have been for the major non-Communist powers of Asia to embark on nuclear-weapons programs. The treaty does allow for underground testing, but testing of this sort would severely complicate the technical and financial problems and would probably be considered a violation of the spirit of the agreement. The Chinese themselves have stated that a nation's first nuclear test must be above ground.[11] As I suggested earlier, the United States is vitally interested in avoiding the proliferation of nuclear weapons and should be willing to undertake major diplomatic moves and military commitments to implement her policy. It is not clear to what extent recognition of that interest and of the desire to prevent nuclear proliferation in Asia entered into the American decision to sign the test ban treaty, but it is clear that the treaty is of value in trying to convince Japan or India not to begin nuclear programs.

In the light of the test ban treaty, what other arms-control agreements (compatible with U.S. defense and other world-wide commitments) might serve the interests of the United

[11] *People's Daily,* August 10, 1963. Translation in *Peking Review,* VI, No. 33 (August 15, 1963), 21.

States in the Pacific in relation to China? The United States has proposed an agreement under which the present nuclear powers would refrain from sharing nuclear information with other countries. Under the test ban treaty, the United States is already committed not to aid other countries in conducting nuclear tests, and this has been interpreted by the American Government as a prohibition against supplying nuclear information to nations planning to carry out nuclear tests—in other words, as an agreement against helping countries to become nuclear powers in their own right.[12] There remains, however, the possibility that the United States would be willing to make a country a nuclear power by giving it finished nuclear weapons, either as a means of circumventing the treaty or, in the case of France, as a means of securing adherence to it. It would be extremely unfortunate if the United States were to decide to give nuclear weapons to nations because they were prohibited by the test ban from developing their own. Just as the test ban may serve to limit the likely spread of nuclear weapons in Asia, so also could a "nonproliferation" agreement serve as a brake, this time by making it illegal for the United States to share her nuclear knowledge with the countries of Asia. There is no likelihood now that the United States is willing to grant weapons, or that any nations would accept them, judging by the support of United Nations General Assembly resolutions against proliferation of nuclear weapons. An international nonproliferation treaty would not only hinder future governments from altering this policy but would also make it easier for the United States to turn down requests for nuclear weapons.

The Chinese have from time to time expressed an interest in nuclear-weapon–free-zone agreements. They have insisted that such agreements would have to include all of the United States and the Soviet Union, and the United States would certainly want to include all of China. There seems to be

12 *Senate Test Ban Hearings,* p. 180.

little prospect of reaching any agreement of this kind, but it may be in the interest of the United States not to oppose agreements on a nuclear-weapon–free zone in the Asian area. Careful consideration of the extent to which American military capability would be impaired by moving weapons out of the Chinese periphery is in order. How quickly could nuclear weapons be returned to the area in the event of large-scale fighting? How effectively can nuclear weapons deployed outside the theater be used? A nuclear-weapon–free Asia may not be to the military disadvantage of the United States.

The United States should refrain from initiating proposals for such zones, since this would suggest that she fears China's development of a nuclear capability and would make it more difficult to station nuclear weapons on Asian territory in the event that no agreement was reached. But there may be political reasons for the United States to support such agreements if they are advocated by other countries.

IMPLICATIONS OF THE SINO-SOVIET DISPUTE

Some of the proposals for American policy that have been made here can be carried out without public discussion, but most of them call for a certain amount of public information and debate—most of which will inevitably be communicated to China and the rest of Asia. Thus it is impossible to separate the articulation of American policy into what the U.S. Government wants Peking to believe and what it wants other Asian governments to believe. Fortunately, there is no divergence between the two. The United States wants China to understand that she will not consider as a serious military force any nuclear capability that China develops within the next several years.

She must state unambiguously that the development of a nuclear weapon will not enhance China's status in the eyes of the United States and that it will not make easier a negotiated settlement of outstanding disputes between Peking and Washington. Here again, the example of France is useful: It should be clear that, while China's adherence to the test ban treaty continues to be welcome, the United States is not prepared to grant major concessions to China to secure her signature.

At the same time that she points out to the Chinese that the political advantage to be gained from building a nuclear force will be limited, the United States should seek to intensify the feeling that danger and insecurity for the Chinese will accompany the development of a Chinese nuclear capability. Since 1949, the Chinese have feared a major American nuclear attack and have planned their policy to avoid such an occurrence. Over the years, they have become less worried about this threat and better able to judge how much they can aid foreign Communist military operations without the United States resorting to the use of nuclear weapons. The Chinese must be made to realize, however, that their development of a nuclear capability will increase rather than decrease the likelihood of the United States using nuclear weapons against them. In the event of renewed hostilities between the United States and the Peking regime in the Taiwan Straits, for example, a Chinese nuclear capability will be a great temptation to a pre-emptive strike: Since any nuclear capability China has in the foreseeable future, although vulnerable, could cause major civilian destruction if used, there will be strong pressure to destroy it at the onset of any overt hostilities. In addition, the United States may imply, there will be pressure from her allies to destroy a Chinese nuclear capability in the event of renewed hostilities—on the Sino-Indian border, for example. Furthermore, the United States should announce to the Chinese that her considerable stake in the principle of forbidding nuclear weapons to be used for political purposes gives her an added incentive to halt Chinese efforts to expand. Chinese use of nuclear weapons would clearly be met, it should be stressed, by a much stronger nuclear capability, which would effectively cancel out any tactical military advantage the Chinese had as well as wreak extensive destruction in China.

None of these arguments is likely to convince the Chinese that they should actually call a stop to their nuclear programs. They are undoubtedly already aware of some of the problems American propaganda brings to their attention—although they probably underestimate, as the French apparently do, the economic and technological costs of an extensive nuclear program. But even if they continue the program, the American policy just outlined should reduce China's expectations of what she can gain from it.

Though the Chinese emphasize the deterrent value of nuclear weapons, there remains the danger that they will launch new acts of aggression—to seize the offshore islands or Taiwan, for example—because they believe that the balance of forces has changed. Undoubtedly, the critical element that led the Chinese in 1957 and 1958 to argue that there had been a fundamental change in the balance of power in the world was the belief on the part of many Americans, if not indeed American officials, that in fact a fundamental change *had* occurred. As Chinese nuclear capability grows, the great danger will be if Peking believes that the American will to resist Chinese aggression has declined. By word as well as deed, the United States must make clear that she is as determined as ever to defend her interests.

The United States will also need to evaluate the continuing efforts of the Chinese to associate the Soviet Union with their defense in the event of an American attack. It is difficult, of course, to assess whether or not the Soviet Union would in fact intervene in the event of an American nuclear attack on Chinese troops or Chinese territory. This will depend on the nature of the attack, to what it was in response, and on the current status of Sino-Soviet relations—in making *any* decision to use nuclear weapons, the United States must carefully consider the possible Soviet reaction. But the American government has probably everything to gain by suggesting to the Chinese what is in fact likely to be the case—that the Soviet Union will not intervene if the United States uses nuclear weapons in response to Chinese aggression unless that use is designed to destroy totally the Communist regime in China. Even then—especially if Sino-Soviet relations have deteriorated, perhaps even to the point of China being read out of the socialist camp—the Soviet Union might not intervene.

An American evaluation of whether the possibility of Soviet intervention or the probability of other factors warrants refraining from using nuclear weapons can only be made at the time and in the given circumstances. Generally, however, the United States should give the impression that she is not convinced that the Soviet Union will intervene. Possibly because of the one difficulty involved in assuming this public posture, which I shall discuss subsequently, the American government has, in fact, taken the opposite line. On April 10, 1963, Secretary of State Dean Rusk, for example, when asked whether the West would capitalize on the Sino-Soviet dispute, replied:

Well, I think that it would be difficult to find major moves that the free world could make which would advance the interests of the free world in trying to insert ourselves in between Moscow and Peking. Because if we ourselves were to, say, increase pressures on one or the other, I think that we could very likely drive these two closer together again.

You see, *neither Moscow nor Peking can afford to be without the other in a direct confrontation between either one of them and the free world.* They are important to each other, and that importance has not been, I think, eliminated by the rivalries that are now apparent within the Communist world. So we have to be a little cautious about this.[13] [Italics added]

13 National Broadcasting Company television interview, reprinted in the U.S. Department of State *Bulletin*, XLVIII, No. 1244 (April 29, 1963), 645.

Even after the events of the summer of 1963, this continued to be the American position. Testifying before the Senate Foreign Relations Committee on the nuclear test ban, Secretary of Defense McNamara had the following exchange with Senator Russell:

> *Senator Russell:* In the event of any threatened hostilities between this country and either China or the Soviet Union, do you not think these countries would get together rather rapidly?
> *Secretary McNamara:* I think we must assume that would be the case and be prepared for it.[14]

One cannot quarrel with McNamara's assertion that the United States must "assume" that China and the Soviet Union would join together if either were involved in hostilities with the United States if by "assume" he meant "take into account the possibility." Certainly the United States must be prepared for such a contingency and take it into account. But the question remains: What should the United States now communicate to the Chinese? It can well be argued that the United States should indicate that she assumes that Russia may not support China in the event of certain kinds of nuclear showdowns. This message need not be directly or formally conveyed to the Chinese, as, for example, in a Presidential speech. But in television and press interviews, legislative hearings, and the like, United States officials could appropriately imply that they question the likelihood of Soviet support of China in the event of an American nuclear attack.

Apart from the general difficulties of separating such public statements from actual contingency planning and cautious unspoken assumptions, there is the specific problem of how to react to Chinese Nationalist demands that the United States support their invasion of the mainland. With the Chinese Nationalist army at the peak of its strength, with the Sino-Soviet rift deepening, and with Communist China turning

[14] *Senate Test Ban Hearings*, p. 112.

her attention to recovery from the economic disaster of the past years, the Nationalists have been arguing that this is the perfect time for the United States to support a landing. One of the main American arguments against giving such support is that it would provoke Soviet intervention. If the United States were to begin to argue that such intervention is not likely, it would be more difficult to refuse support to the Nationalists. However, although this factor does need to be taken into account, it does not seem to be of overriding importance. In the face of only informal and "unofficial" statements about the improbability of Russian intervention, the Nationalists would find it hard to re-open the argument in a serious way. Moreover, the United States has another and very substantial reason for refusing to support a Chinese Nationalist invasion —specifically, that it is very likely to fail.

On balance, therefore, the prospects are favorable for a carefully calculated campaign of statements implying that the U.S. Government, because of the growing Sino-Soviet dispute and because of American nuclear superiority, doubts whether the Soviet Union will come to the aid of China in the event of American nuclear attack. The statements should stress that such an attack would be possible in reaction to Chinese aggression—in order to avoid provoking the fears that the United States is about to initiate nuclear war. Statements by the President or other high officials should be avoided, since they might force the Soviet Union into declaring her readiness to defend China, as she did in June, 1962, when both President Kennedy and Premier Khrushchev made statements about the Chinese Communist build-up across from Taiwan. Such a campaign can be carried on successfully only if American officials make it clear, as they should, that they find it significantly probable that the Soviet Union would remain aloof from certain kinds of Sino-American wars, even nuclear wars.

Undoubtedly the Chinese will pick up any messages of this

kind even if they are conveyed through Congressional testimony or in other seemingly out-of-the-way places. There is ample evidence in the Chinese press that this material is carefully read and digested in Peking; it finds its way to speeches and statements by leaders of the regime as well as to more general propaganda. But it may also be advisable to communicate some kind of message via the Sino-American talks that take place periodically in Warsaw. This probably should be done indirectly and by implication, if at all, in talking about the Sino-Soviet dispute or perhaps in urging the Chinese to sign the test ban treaty, rather than as a nuclear military threat.

Particularly if the Sino-Soviet relationship veers in the direction of a complete split, such as in the summer of 1963, the United States might well wish to explore with the Soviet Union the possibility of joint action to halt the Chinese nuclear program or to render it politically and militarily useless. The Soviet Union now seems prepared to talk openly with official and unofficial American representatives about the Chinese danger. Certainly, their propaganda dispute with the Chinese rests partly on the argument that the Chinese believe in nuclear war and are prepared to risk the destruction of millions of lives in order to secure their objectives. It may be possible for the United States to raise quietly with the Soviet Union the questions of what the world should do about the growing threat from China and whether there is not some basis for joint action.[15]

The most extreme form of joint Soviet-American action (or unilateral action by one or the other) would be a military move designed to destroy Chinese nuclear facilities. The number of locations that would have to be destroyed is small, and destruction could be carried out quickly, certainly if nuclear weapons were used and possibly with conventional bombs or

[15] Several press reports have suggested that the United States made such an approach to the Soviet Union at the time of the signing of the test ban treaty in July, 1963, and was rebuffed by Soviet leaders. (See *The New York Times*, October 2, 1964, p. 3; *The Washington Post*, October 2, 1964, p. A 21.)

sabotage (perhaps by the Chinese Nationalists). If the Soviet Union should ever reach the point where she was prepared to make such a move, the United States should indicate that she has no objection to it and will not interfere in any way.

But the United States needs also to consider the possibility of military action to destroy the Chinese nuclear power undertaken on her own initiative. Stewart Alsop has proposed that the nation should take whatever military steps are necessary to prevent the Chinese from developing a nuclear capability—in fact he asserts that the American Government has already made this decision—on the grounds that the Chinese are "maniacs" who are likely to behave irresponsibly when they get nuclear weapons.[16] If, however, one believes that the Chinese are responsible and calculating, then the case for trying to destroy their nuclear production plants must be based on the argument that in the long run a substantial Chinese capability will gravely threaten American security and increase the likelihood of nuclear war. Many objections to the proposal nevertheless come to mind, but it would still appear to deserve careful study.

One key question has already been alluded to: Are the Soviets likely to remain aloof if the United States in fact destroys the Chinese nuclear capability? Careful and private soundings of the Russians might well provide some clue to the answer. The more subtle and clandestine the attack, and the more clearly directed against only the nuclear production facilities of China, the easier it might be for the Soviet Union to make nothing more than verbal and diplomatic protests. What military moves the Soviet would carry out if they did intervene is another key consideration. It would hardly make sense to launch an all-out war against the United States in response to a carefully limited American attack on a Chinese

16 Stewart Alsop, "Affairs of State: The Real Meaning of the Test Ban," *Saturday Evening Post*, September 28, 1963, p. 20. See also Robert S. Allen and Paul Scott, "Peking Due to Test Soon," *Newport News Times-Herald*, September 19, 1964.

military capability that the Soviets had been arguing was unnecessary and in fact dangerous. If one questions whether the United States would risk New York to save parts of Western Europe, it is absurd to assume that the Soviet Union would be prepared to risk Moscow and in fact all of Russia to defend China's right to a nuclear capability, particularly since the American nuclear superiority is still overwhelming. It is lesser interventions that cannot be ruled out—including a possible Soviet move against existing French nuclear facilities. The Soviet Union might even transfer nuclear weapons to the Chinese for use in retaliation against American attack, but one cannot tell how they would be used or whether the Soviets would really want to give such weapons when they could not avoid helping the Chinese in problems of bomb design, etc., for a renewed nuclear program. Not even the Soviet leaders themselves can predict what their reaction would be to the destruction of China's nuclear force, but it is certain that such an attack would always be fraught with the danger of leading to general nuclear war. Nevertheless, that danger could be minimized by other accompanying military and diplomatic moves.

The political and moral arguments against such an attack remain strong, however. There would be much opposition to it among allies and neutrals in Asia; America's European allies would see it as a reckless move confirming the belief that the American government cannot be trusted with the leadership of the Western alliance; and it is debatable whether a strike against China—like destruction of Soviet missiles in Cuba without any warning, which some proposed—is compatible with the moral standards of the United States. In addition, such an attack would not permanently prevent China from becoming a nuclear power and might force the United States into even greater attacks on China in an effort to suppress her determination to become a nuclear power. Finally, there is the technical military question of how the Chinese nuclear production capability could be destroyed and how effectively this would halt or substantially set back the Chinese nuclear program. This depends in part on the kind of nuclear production plants the Chinese have, whether the United States knows their precise location, and whether these targets are close to American military bases or far away. Politically, the most advantageous and least dangerous method of eliminating them would be sabotage, which could appear to be carried out by indigenous or Chinese Nationalist forces sent from Taiwan. At the other extreme would be open American nuclear bombardment, perhaps preceded by an ultimatum to the Chinese to close down their production plants and sign the test ban treaty.

Certainly, no definitive answer to the question of whether the United States should try to halt the Chinese nuclear program by military force can be given here. All that can be urged is that the problem be given careful detailed consideration at the highest level of government, remembering that a number of years from now we may have reasons to regret not having weighed the possibility at this time.[17]

If, as seems likely, the United States either does not consider the possibility of a military move against China or, having considered it rejects it, one must weigh the measures short of military force that can be brought to bear against the Chinese to halt their nuclear program. An American propaganda campaign making clear that the risk of American nuclear attack will increase when China becomes a nuclear power and

[17] With the benefit of hindsight, we may now question whether the United States should have decided to eliminate the Soviet capability in the immediate postwar period. There are, of course, substantial differences between the situation then and the situation now with China, particularly the facts that then the American stockpile was very small and the Soviet Union could threaten to overrun Western Europe if attacked. The current American stockpile is large enough to prevent massive conventional retaliation by the Chinese, but there exists another nuclear power—the Soviet Union—capable of intervening. My expectation is that the United States Government, if it carefully considered the question, would still decide not to try to prevent China by military means from developing a nuclear capability.

that nuclear power will not enhance China's prestige might have some effect. Military and diplomatic moves taken in co-ordination, even if tacitly, with the Soviet bloc might help. Economic pressures of various kinds could be applied, including, from the Soviet side, cutting off oil shipments. A blockade specifically aimed at making a Chinese nuclear explosion impossible is not feasible, but a blockade could hamper efforts to develop delivery systems, particularly if they are able now to acquire from any source long-range bombers or civilian planes that can be converted into long-range bombers. A more general economic blockade would appear difficult to organize and unlikely to succeed. In the short run it would not be successful and in the long run difficult to maintain. Even cutting off Soviet oil supplies, which have apparently already been reduced, would not have a decisive impact. Therefore, in one way or another, short of direct military action, the United States must be prepared to react at some time within the 1960's or 1970's to a Chinese nuclear force.

6

A Modest Chinese Nuclear Capability

ANY QUALITATIVE DISTINCTION between various degrees of nuclear capability must be arbitrary. There are no clear breaks in the progression from the initial decision to establish a military nuclear-weapons program to the development of the kind of sophisticated nuclear force now possessed by the United States or the Soviet Union. Nevertheless, in analyzing the implications of China's developing a nuclear capability, it seems useful to consider first, a "modest" and, second, a "major" capability—a "modest" capability being defined as one able to deliver a small number of weapons (from twenty to thirty) against China's neighbors, and a "major" capability being a force able to deliver a dozen or more fusion weapons at intercontinental range. This chapter deals with the possibility of China developing a modest capability.

In evaluating any military force equipped with nuclear weapons it is necessary to consider the available weapons, the delivery systems that are used, the countries to be attacked or threatened, their proximity to the delivery systems, and whatever defenses these nations have against the nuclear forces. The first delivery systems China organizes may be extremely crude, with fission weapons small enough to put in the very few Badger or more advanced Bear supersonic bombers the Russians have probably given them. It is more likely that China will have to depend on the Soviet T.U. 4 bomber (Bull) and the I.L. 28 light bombers (Beagles) of which, according to several reports, she has received fairly large numbers.[1] At a somewhat later day, the Chinese will no doubt have medium-range missiles mated with their first nuclear (fusion) warheads—delivery systems that are extremely unsophisticated and vulnerable to pre-emptive first strikes. The United States knows the location of virtually all the major Chinese air bases now, and will quickly discover the location of any missile sites. Since in the foreseeable future the Chinese probably will not have sophisticated radar and warning systems to help them get their bombers or missiles off the ground quickly in response to indications of an imminent American missile attack, the United States would be able at any time to destroy China's entire delivery capability. Thus, whatever modest capability the Chinese will acquire by the late 1960's or early 1970's will be of doubtful value against sophisticated defense systems and will be susceptible to American pre-emption.

Still, the chance that China could successfully employ a nuclear weapon against enemy forces cannot be ruled out. For example, China will eventually be able to deliver a nuclear weapon against Indian ground forces along the Sino-Indian border or against one of the offshore islands occupied by the

---

[1] See, for example, Beaton and Maddox, *The Spread of Nuclear Weapons*, p. 126, and the Institute for Strategic Studies, *The Military Balance 1963–1964* (London, 1963), p. 10.

Chinese Nationalists. They may be able to create the impression—whether misleading or not—that they can, for example, destroy Tokyo. In addition, unorthodox means of delivery—by ship, for instance, to blow up a harbor—cannot be ruled out, either as a possible maneuver in a situation of great desperation, or because fear of such action may be significant in a country with vulnerable port cities. How great the actual military threat that a modest Chinese capability could be, then, will vary, first over time—for China's capability will increase in sophistication and size—and second, with the particular country concerned.

Political Exploitation of a Nuclear Force

As they did at the time of the detonation of their first nuclear device, the Chinese will probably continue for some time to underplay the role of their nuclear weapons. They may simply demonstrate what military capability they have, perhaps exaggerate its power, but it is unlikely that they will make any specific threats of specific use of their forces. Demonstrating their actual nuclear capability will not be as easy as it was to prove they could explode a nuclear device. The Chinese could resort to a well-publicized test of a nuclear weapon dropped from an airplane, but this involves many difficult technical problems, not to mention the possibility, however remote, that the bomb might not go off and the difficulty of proving to other countries that the test took place. In addition, it would be difficult, if not impossible, to prove that such a weapon could penetrate enemy defenses. When they eventually develop missiles, the Chinese Communist regime will very likely test them publicly, perhaps inviting military attachés stationed in Peking to view the tests.

The political use to which China will put her developing nuclear capability is likely to be general, within the context of her claim to being a great power whose views cannot be ignored in the settlement of Asian or disarmament and arms-control problems. She can base her right to participate in international conferences or to be recognized as having an important part in the settlement of disputes on the fact that she is now one of the world's five nuclear powers; she can then attribute whatever success she does attain in political conferences at least partly to the fact that she has a nuclear capability. Just as Great Britain, for example, tends to justify her independent nuclear force partly on the grounds that it provides access for disarmament and other negotiations, so China, if she does succeed in entering international negotiations of any kind, is likely to attribute her success to her nuclear power. This will be done, as it was in Britain, to justify, both in the domestic and international sphere, the development of nuclear weapons—to emphasize that the purpose of becoming a nuclear power is to enhance China's ability to influence peacefully the settlement of international disputes in Asia.

The possession of a modest nuclear force will give China new means for playing on the fears of her Asian neighbors. As that force grows, she will be able to claim with more and more justification that she is the dominant military power in Asia, and hence entitled to a say in the foreign policy of the small nations on her borders. Already she has gained hegemony over some of her neighbors. With the additional prestige of nuclear weapons, China will probably continue this policy—a combination of relatively mild implicit threats and promises to respect the territorial integrity of her neighbors—in the hopes of consolidating her political influence in South and Southeast Asia. Political groups in the Asian nations that argue against coming to terms with Communist China will find it more difficult to do so when Peking can claim to be the only indigenous nuclear power in the Far East. The threat she poses will be clearer to all concerned, and the choice between accepting Chinese hegemony or closely allying with the United States will be posed more sharply. But the pressures to go in one or the other direction may in some countries tend to cancel each other out and lead to an affirmation of neutrality.

The Chinese Communist regime could, of course, suggest that its nuclear capability was developed for the protection of all Asia against American aggression. The Chinese are likely to appeal to Asian anti-Western feelings by arguing that it is impermissible that the control of nuclear weapons remain in the hands of Western powers alone, and that the People's Republic is acting for all Asia in developing a nuclear force which will prevent the assertion of neo-colonialism in the area —that China will never use nuclear weapons first or against an Asian country but developed the weapons purely for China's self-defense. China might also imply that the weapons could be used to defend other nations prepared to enter into defensive alliance with her against Western imperialism. Depending on other political factors, an appeal of this kind might have some attraction, for example, to Indonesia, should she be seeking to extend her area of control in continued opposition to Malaysia or to Australian control of East New Guinea. Whether or not the Indonesians are prepared to make any kind of direct alliance with the Chinese, the Chinese could on their own initiative indicate that their military force, including their nuclear arms, was available if requested in this kind of a dispute; if the Indonesian policy succeeded, they would later be in a position to claim that their help had been crucial. Wherever disputes occur in Asia—as, for example, the Pakistani-Indian quarrel over Kashmir—China may look for a chance to intervene—presenting herself as the champion of Asian interests who had developed a nuclear capability purely for this purpose.

The continued existence of the Chinese Nationalist regime on Taiwan provides another theme on which the Chinese Communists can play in explaining their decision to develop an independent nuclear capability. Peking can maintain that as long as a foreign power—i.e., the United States—"occupies" some of their territory and threatens to help a counter-revolutionary group to return to power, they have no recourse but to develop *all* the means necessary for defense.

Finally, the Chinese can continue with the line they adopted immediately after the three-environment test-ban treaty was signed and following the detonation of their first bomb—of calling for general nuclear disarmament. Nuclear testing, they can say, is necessary to put China on a par with the aggressive imperialists and non-Asian socialist powers, but they are quite willing to abandon a testing program whenever the other nuclear powers are willing to destroy all of their nuclear weapons. They may press for participation in whatever disarmament talks are currently taking place and renew their proposals for a conference of all nations aimed at the abolition of nuclear weapons. They could also press a general "peace offensive" by proposing both regional arms control agreements and political settlements of disputes in Indochina and elsewhere in Asia.

Recognizing the political difficulties that China's nuclear capability can create among groups throughout Asia who are vigorously opposed to nuclear weapons but otherwise generally sympathetic to her cause, the Chinese must obviously provide as many justifications as they can for their nuclear program, in terms that help to cement rather than to disrupt relations with their Asian neighbors. The other side of the coin—the greater threat that China will pose when she possesses nuclear weapons and therefore the need to come to terms with her as a potential aggressor—may well be unmentioned by the Chinese; elites in other Asian countries can be expected to note the threat. However, specific military threats may be made particularly against regimes lacking wide support, such as the Chinese Nationalist government on Taiwan, and against Japan as long as she is an ally of the United States.

The United States and the Soviet Union: Responses to China's Threat

The United States' political response to a modest Chinese nuclear capability need not diverge from the line taken at the time of the initial Chinese nuclear detonation—stress on the limited military significance of the Chinese capability and on the enormous sacrifice that nuclear armaments required of the Chinese people and the Chinese economy, warnings of the danger to world peace posed by China's insistence on continuing with a nuclear program. The United States should continue to emphasize that China's signing of the test ban treaty must precede any more extensive arms-control negotiations between Washington and Peking. The United States should also reconfirm her willingness to meet defense commitments in Asia and her ability to do so, if necessary without recourse to nuclear weapons, reiterating that if China threatens or tries to use nuclear weapons against any of her neighbors, the United States has the capability to retaliate with overwhelming nuclear strength.

China will have difficulty in any case in calling attention to her nuclear force, and the United States should not help her to do so by stressing the Chinese capability or by giving it a prominent role in propaganda campaigns in Asia. Rather, the United States should attempt to portray the Chinese nuclear capability as a relatively unimportant factor on the Asian scene and should emphasize her positive commitment to prevent Asia from coming under Communist control and to improve the economic and social conditions of the people— a line of reasoning that is compatible with encouraging opposition to China's nuclear efforts. She can point to the example Japan and India set in renouncing the need for nuclear arms and accepting the test ban treaty. And, as the Chinese continue their development of nuclear weapons, conducting the necessary additional nuclear tests, each one of these can be a suitable occasion for American condemnation, and for American efforts to associate other Asian states with her effort to persuade China to abandon the testing and sign the treaty. The American Government should emphasize that it is willing to consider other arms-control arrangements in the Far East only after China has halted her testing of nuclear weapons.

The United States program of providing allied and neutral nations with technical information indicating the limits of the Chinese capability is worth continuing. Insofar as protection of intelligence sources permits, the United States could also share with the nations of Asia, to some extent publicly and in more detail privately, her current evaluation of Chinese nuclear development—the number of bombs the Chinese have, what sort of vehicles they have for delivering them. As she did in the pre-detonation and immediate post-detonation periods, the United States could quietly remind Asia of her extensive nuclear force in the Pacific theater and her ability to respond quickly to Chinese use of nuclear weapons. The United States should reaffirm any specific commitment she has made with an Asian nation to respond, if requested, to China's use of nuclear weapons by an attack of equal or greater force.

The continuation of the Sino-Soviet conflict will help the United States to make credible this willingness to aid a country attacked by Chinese nuclear weapons. For the United States can point out that China has no nuclear capability to attack the United States and hence that the United States would not put her own territory in jeopardy were she to attack China; that the United States does not believe the Soviet Union, which does have such forces, would come to the aid of China should the United States retaliate for her use of nuclear weapons. Every effort should be made to publicize the disparity in military power between the United States and a China not allied to the Soviet Union.

If Sino-Soviet relations continue to deteriorate, the Soviet

Union may be willing to publish information to verify the limitations of the Chinese nuclear force, for she undoubtedly has accurate information about the kind of delivery systems the Chinese were working on at least until 1960, and could, if she so desired, confirm the American assertion of their limited capability. If the Soviets condemn Chinese nuclear explosions when they occur, and make it clear that they hope Peking will sign the test ban treaty, they will strengthen the view that they are not prepared to come to the defense of China, particularly if the Chinese are the first to use nuclear weapons.

The Sino-Soviet split also makes possible tacit Soviet-American cooperation in the defense of Asian countries against Chinese threats. In the fall of 1963, before China made claim to be a nuclear power, the Soviet Union was already giving signs that she was prepared to provide military assistance to nations threatened by China. The Soviet Union concluded an arms agreement that called for her supplying an unspecified but considerable amount of military assistance to the Indian Government, clearly for use on the Sino-Indian border. In addition, after negotiations in Moscow, Russia agreed to supply military assistance in Laos to the neutralist forces of Kong Le, for use against the Viet Cong guerrillas supported by the North Vietnamese and the Chinese. In both cases, the decisions to give aid seem to have been made after careful deliberation and much negotiation, and to reflect a well-thought-out and firm trend in Soviet policy. This trend is likely to continue when China develops a modest nuclear capability, and may be accelerated. The Soviet Union, indeed, may be willing to give guaranties against Chinese nuclear aggression, at least privately, to certain governments, such as in India, and they may be willing to supply defensive military equipment—although almost certainly without nuclear warheads—to use against Chinese aggression.

This component of Soviet policy poses fundamental problems for the United States, requiring that American attitudes to the Cold War and about international politics in the postwar period be revised. For some time after the victory of the Communist regime in China, the United States approached Asia in the same terms as she did Europe: as an area in which the United States and her allies confront a monolithic Communist bloc controlled from Moscow, assuming that any aggressive action by a Communist state met with at least the tacit approval of the Soviet Government. In forming multilateral alliances such as SEATO or signing bilateral defense agreements with Japan, the Chinese Nationalist government on Taiwan, the Philippines, and Korea, the United States did not distinguish between China and Russia, on the premise that the threat from the two countries was a single one the response to which could be summed up as "opposing international Communism." Clearly this is no longer the case. In Asia in fact, the United States may begin to find herself more and more often tacitly allied with the Soviet Union against Chinese aggression. The United States will find that Asian nations are willing to accept American military assistance against China while remaining on friendly terms with the Soviet Union and in fact receiving assistance from her. It is important that the American Government recognize and accommodate itself to these new possibilities and problems. The United States should recognize, for example, that the Indian Government *has* been able to maintain a policy of nonalignment in the Soviet-American conflict, while accepting large quantities of American and Soviet military equipment to meet the threat from China. Similarly, the efforts of the "neutral" faction in Laos to maintain its neutrality has been enhanced by the willingness of the Soviet Union and the United States to supply aid for the struggle against the Pathet Lao. The United States Government may soon find that it has no choice but to accept this ambiguity in the Cold War and to seize what advantage she can from tacit alignment with the Soviet Union.

As China develops her nuclear capability, the feeling on the part of Asian countries that the Soviet Union is willing to oppose Chinese aggression will be very important in their decision whether or not they must accept Chinese hegemony or develop their own nuclear forces. Assuming that the United States continues, as she should, to oppose both these policies, it may be desirable that these nations feel that they can count on both the Soviet Union and the United States for support. Such a situation would complicate the moral issues of the Cold War and undoubtedly create difficulties in the American Congress and among certain sectors of American public opinion; more important, it would significantly enhance Soviet prestige and influence in Asia. But the United States may have no choice: Many Asian countries are determined to remain neutral in the Soviet-American conflict, but at the same time they recognize that they face a real threat of aggression from China and her Communist allies in Asia. If the United States exploits rather than opposes nonalignment, separate but parallel Soviet and American arrangements may be possible to guarantee the countries on the borders of China against Chinese military action. Even with this dual protection, however, the threat will remain a serious one. The United States will have to deal with the particular military threats that are made on a country-by-country basis.

Defense Against the Threat of Nuclear Weapons

In considering the kind of aid and advice that the United States can and should give to nations that feel themselves threatened by the growth of a Chinese nuclear capability, a number of factors must be considered. While no attempt is made here to consider every nation of Asia or every possible use to which nuclear or other weapons might be put, several illustrations can serve to suggest the type of policy the United States can adopt to meet the threats of nuclear warfare in Asia.

Taiwan

Probably the most acute problem for American foreign policy in Asia, vis-à-vis a Communist China armed with a modest nuclear capability, will be what to do about the Chinese Nationalist regime on Taiwan; the Peking regime may threaten explicitly to use nuclear weapons in the event that the Nationalists seek to return to the mainland. This threat must be taken seriously by the United States; it will add to the already overwhelming arguments against "unleashing" Chiang Kai-shek's forces. It will also, however, further undermine the morale of the Taiwan regime by making it even clearer that the prospects for a return to the mainland are low. And it may generate pressure on the United States from the Taiwan regime to make a pre-emptive strike against the Chinese Communist nuclear capability in order to clear the way for a return to the mainland and to eliminate the aggressive use of Chinese Communist nuclear weapons against Taiwan or the offshore islands. In all, China's possession of a modest nuclear capability may well add to other pressures which suggest that the United States should move in the direction of a "two-China" solution. In the end, it may be necessary to disavow any intention to support the Kuomintang's return to the mainland. The United States may be forced to stress her previously stated position that: (1) she was not prepared to support the use of force to enable the Nationalists to return to the mainland; and (2) the Chiang Kai-shek regime had in fact committed itself in 1958 not to use force to regain control of mainland China.

Besides threatening to use nuclear weapons defensively against a Nationalist invasion, the Peking regime may implicitly or explicitly threaten to use nuclear weapons against Nationalist-held territory—either the offshore islands of Quemoy and Matsu or Taiwan itself. With even a very modest capability, the Chinese Communists could deliver a nuclear weapon against the Quemoy islands or Matsu by aircraft or possibly by boat, and no form of air defense could make this impossible. Given the uncertainty of American policy in relation to the defense of these islands, it would be difficult to counter any Communist threat to use nuclear weapons against them. It should be pointed out to Chiang Kai-shek that nothing can be done to protect the one-third of his combat forces he has kept stationed on Quemoy since the mid-1950's.

By contrast, American guarantees for the defense of Taiwan against Communist nuclear attack must be made firmer. The Nationalist air force has shown that it is more than a match for the Chinese Communist forces—even when, as in 1958, Peking was receiving extensive aid from the Soviet Union. The reduction of Soviet aid—including supplies of spare parts and refined fuel—can only have served to reduce the efficiency and effectiveness of the Chinese Communist air force. Given the limited Communist capability, the Nationalists themselves may be able to defend Taiwan against an attempted nuclear attack; certainly, a combination of American and Chinese Nationalist air-to-air and surface-to-air missile defenses should effectively repel any attempt by Communist China to penetrate the territory of Taiwan with a nuclear-armed aircraft. The defenses of Taiwan are apparently already adequate to defend the island against Chinese Communist attack with manned aircraft, and the United States has every reason sympathetically to accede to requests for strengthening Taiwan's air defense system as China's nuclear capability develops. For the system must be much more reliable and must be able to destroy a much larger percentage of the attacking force if the latter is armed with atomic weapons. The United States may want to make Taiwan a showcase for the effectiveness of air defense systems as a means of neutralizing the crude Chinese Communist delivery capability. Since the Nationalist regime is unlikely to hesitate to accept nuclear weapons under American or dual control, it should be possible to establish an excellent defense system for the island that could serve as a model for the system the United States would be prepared to deploy in India, Japan, or elsewhere.

Thus China's development of a modest nuclear capability could well dash the Nationalist hopes to return to the mainland—and therefore create a political crisis on Taiwan that would be resolved only by the formation of a regime frankly resigned to accept permanently the status of Government of Taiwan. At the same time, the regime on Taiwan could be adequately protected against a nuclear threat from the mainland, especially if it were prepared to withdraw from the offshore islands. Chinese Communist nuclear capability may serve as the means to shift American policy in a direction that seems for other reasons to be desirable.

India

It is in India that it is most likely that some sort of Soviet-American cooperation for defense against China's nuclear threats will be possible. This cooperation, however, would raise not only the political problems previously discussed but technical security problems concerning the operations of American anti-aircraft and later anti-missile defensive systems. It remains to be seen whether some procedure can be worked out that will allow the Indians to receive equipment which presumably requires the presence of technical advisers from both the United States and the Soviet Union, without either or both donors feeling that their defense systems against each other have been compromised. The Indians should be encouraged to obtain military aid and military commitments from the Soviet Union just short of the point where it would no longer be prudent for the United States to supply India with military equipment or perhaps to establish a joint British-American-Indian air defense system.

In the case of India, however, no defense system in operation now or believed to be possible in the future can guarantee with absolute certainty the destruction of all weapons launched by the Chinese. It is considerably more difficult to defend all of India than it is to defend the small island of Taiwan, and some Indian troops in the border areas and some Indian cities would remain exposed to destruction by a Chinese nuclear weapon. It should be recalled that in the fall of 1962, the Indian Government was intensely concerned with the possibility of Peking's conventional bombing of the civilian population, and it was reluctant to employ air power in the border-area battle zone, for fear that the Chinese would retaliate by attacking an Indian city. Though the Indians may well recognize that Chinese use of nuclear weapons would lead to retaliation in kind by the United States and perhaps by the Soviet Union, they would also have to reckon with the terrible impact of large-scale destruction of Indian cities by the Chinese. It may be difficult, therefore, to convince the Indian government that it should continue its resolute opposition to the Chinese Communists.

Though she can do nothing to eliminate the *possibility* of large-scale civilian damage (in the pre-"megadeath" sense in which Asians still rightly think), the United States may still choose to urge the Indian Government to establish an extensive air defense that could destroy at least most incoming Chinese weapons. For this purpose, it may be important to give the Indians a detailed and realistic picture of the kind of delivery systems the Chinese have and the ability of sophisticated radar and surface-to-air defense systems to combat their capability.

Japan

The Japanese Government is likely to react with mixed feelings to China's development of a nuclear capability and her continued unwillingness to sign the test ban treaty. The

Japanese Government and public are particularly sensitive on the nuclear-arms issue, and Japan would find it difficult to establish friendlier relations than at present with a regime that tests nuclear weapons and makes at least implicit nuclear threats. At the same time, there will be increased fear of China within Japan, and more weight given to the argument that Japan must in some way seek an understanding with the military giant developing close to her shores. Japan's commitment to the alliance with the United States is likely to remain firm, however, despite these new and growing anxieties. Here again, the United States should always make known her commitment to the defense of Japan, as expressed in the Japanese-American Mutual Security Treaty, and her actual physical ability to defend Japan against primitive Chinese delivery systems.

The development of an effective air defense system against the Chinese nuclear capability can bring to the fore, however, the continuing issue of the stationing of American nuclear forces on Japanese territory. Thus far, the Japanese have successfully resisted any suggestion that nuclear weapons be placed on their territory, even for defensive purposes. Any Japanese government that did accept nuclear weapons would be subjected to bitter and widespread opposition—so much so as to imperil the Japanese-American alliance and to hamper any efforts to bring Japan more closely into political, conventional, and anti-guerrilla operations in Asia. It is therefore questionable whether the United States should even try to persuade the Japanese to accept nuclear warheads on their territory. Whether she does or not would depend very largely on the technical military question, which cannot be evaluated here, of how important it is to have nuclear warheads on the surface-to-air missiles or nuclear bombs on the jet fighters that would be committed directly to Japan's defense. A comparison should be made of the efficiencies of a force stationed in Japan and equipped with nuclear weapons and a force that depended on conventional forces stationed in Japan and nuclear forces stationed in Okinawa and on ships in the Pacific. If careful consideration shows that the stationing of nuclear weapons in Japan would make a significant difference, then it might be worth trying to press the Japanese government on this question, but the political risks of doing so and the political cost to any Japanese government of accepting should be recognized and carefully weighed.

Indochina

In relation to Indochina—and, in fact, to the other countries on the Chinese border—the possible use of nuclear weapons must be seen largely in tactical rather than strategic terms. These countries may well fear that the United States will be more reluctant to send troops to defend them against conventional attacks when this could lead to a nuclear war with China involving the death of American troops. By way of countering this fear, the United States must stress that China will have, for a long time, only a very limited number of nuclear weapons and will probably be unwilling to use them for limited tactical military purposes; that the risks involved in using nuclear weapons at all are so great that Peking is unlikely to use them for the purpose of winning a single battle; and that the United States' own supply of tactical nuclear weapons is much larger and could be used effectively against any Chinese attempt at local military victory. Furthermore, China's threat will continue to be largely one of political subversion, and the United States' willingness to provide counter-assistance at this level should effectively check a Chinese threat of large-scale conventional intervention paving the way for tactical nuclear threats.

Most of all, however, it must be realized that the possibility of Chinese intervention in local conflicts will be reduced insofar as her possession of nuclear weapons will lead her to fear American nuclear power more. Peking *with* the bomb should be pictured as more circumspect in its commitment of large-scale conventional forces—which American tactical nuclear forces could readily destroy and which could provoke an American strategic nuclear strike against the Chinese mainland.

There seems to be no reason to press, therefore, for the stationing of tactical nuclear weapons in these nations: Any nuclear action can be carried out from American planes stationed on carriers of the Seventh Fleet, and in general it seems advisable to limit the spread of nuclear weapons even under dual control only to places where such weapons are in fact necessary—for example, for air defense.

CHINESE EMPLOYMENT OF A MODEST NUCLEAR CAPABILITY

As stated earlier, the Chinese will probably never have the opportunity successfully to employ their modest nuclear capability. They will perhaps comprehend this and refrain from using nuclear weapons even as their capability develops and becomes more sophisticated. They may also be deterred by those political pressures and fear of escalation into large-scale war that have deterred both the United States and the Soviet Union from employing nuclear weapons. In addition, the Chinese will undoubtedly recognize their vast inferiority to the United States in tactical and strategic nuclear weapons and hence not move beyond the point of threats—possibly explicit, but more likely implicit—to use nuclear weapons in the event of American aggressions. The Chinese motives for developing nuclear weapons do not in any sense impel them to use these weapons or even plan to use them at any time in the near future. To suggest that the Chinese will forego employing nuclear weapons is not to suggest that their nuclear program does not make sense to them.

No realistic analyst of the Asian scene would dismiss outright, however, the possibility of China using her modest nuclear capability. Thought must be given in advance to the likely results and reactions. There seems to be no question but that the United States should react promptly to any Chinese use of nuclear weapons: The entire American position in the Far East would be untenable if the United States permitted the Chinese to employ nuclear weapons successfully against an Asian opponent. What form does the retaliation take? Certainly, as a preliminary step, the United States should make every effort to know the location of all Chinese air bases, and missile bases when they exist, so that they can be rapidly destroyed if necessary. It may in fact be advisable to reveal to the Chinese that the United States possesses this information. For in the event of China making fairly large-scale use of nuclear weapons against, for example, Indian cities, there seems to be little doubt that the United States should retaliate massively to destroy China's nuclear capability. There is also a strong case for similar action in the event of even a limited tactical use of Chinese nuclear weapons against Indian troops, for example, or against the Nationalists in the Taiwan Straits. Nevertheless, in such a situation, it may be desirable to respond on the tactical level, at least initially, making it clear that the reciprocal use of tactical nuclear weapons can only work to the disadvantage of the Chinese Communists.

Given that the United States can and should destroy the Chinese ability to deliver nuclear weapons if the Chinese employ nuclear weapons against another Asian country, there remains the question of whether the United States should destroy other targets at the same time. As the result of uncertainty about the precise location of the nuclear weapons and the planes that can deliver them, the United States might be obliged to destroy all Chinese airfields within range of the nation under attack, in addition to any presumed missile sites and missile test sites. It might be desirable at that point at

least to consider a further nuclear attack on military and industrial installations in China—so as to destroy her power of
offensive military action. The possibility of altering the political leadership in China will also arise as a possible consequence of large nuclear attacks.

Should a tense political crisis develop in which the Chinese
use of nuclear weapons begins to appear possible, the United
States might well want to canvass Asian countries as well as
the Soviet Union as to their estimate of how they will react to
such a massive nuclear attack on China. Three factors will
ultimately determine whether such an attack makes sense:
the political reaction of other Asian states, the technical problems of such an attack and the number of civilian casualties
that would ensue, and the estimated Soviet reaction and
whether it would lead to general nuclear war. However, it
may be that an attack only on all of China's possible nuclear
delivery centers (possibly also the communication centers
that go with them) would be sufficient to bring about at least
a change in the Communist leadership if not an overthrow of
the Communist regime.

It is most likely that China will use nuclear weapons in
such a way as to be clearly construed as a defensive action
against a Nationalist invasion of the mainland. Such a situation would pose grave political risks for the United States.
For a variety of reasons, the United States has been unwilling
to support a Chinese Nationalist push to the mainland and
will probably still be after the Peking regime acquires a nuclear capability. But the Nationalists may reach a point of
desperation—knowing they must act before their army begins
to decline in efficiency, before Chiang Kai-shek dies, and
before the Chinese nuclear capability grows—and launch an
attack without American support. At this stage, the Chinese
Communists might decide that the necessity of destroying the
landing force as quickly as possible required them to use the
nuclear weapons on Chinese territory. Certainly this might be

the case if the Nationalists had succeeded in acquiring control over a relatively large area that could be devastated with kiloton weapons. It is impossible to indicate in advance what the American reaction to such a series of events should be, but it is clear that the United States Government should do everything in its power to avoid having to face such a dilemma. For if this series of events were to occur nonetheless, the United States would be torn between her desire not to permit use of nuclear weapons and her unwillingness to object to what all Asians and many Americans will view as a justifiable use of nuclear weapons in defense of one's homeland against an enemy invasion. In that sort of situation, it would not be desirable to launch a nuclear attack on the Chinese mainland. The best that could be done would be to help the remaining Nationalist forces evacuate from the mainland and to persuade them at last to resign themselves to governing over Taiwan alone.

ARMS CONTROL

Along with increased fear of China and the consequent attempt of some Asian nations independently to come to terms with China as she builds her nuclear capability, there will be a growing demand in Asia and throughout the world for a comprehensive political settlement with China that would, hopefully, bring her within the framework of the nuclear test ban and that would eliminate the overt hostility between the United States and the Peking regime. The United States will have to cope with these pressures and be willing to consider plans for *détente* advanced by Asian powers as well as negotiations with the Chinese. As for the latter, the United States should state publicly that she has been meeting continuously with the Chinese in Warsaw, that she is prepared as always to continue to do so and to negotiate there any possible settlement of Sino-American differences, but that she will not be forced into concessions by the development of a primitive Chinese nuclear capability. The American Government should stress that the first steps must be China's renunciation of force for the settlement of disputes in the Taiwan Straits. Once and if this step is taken, the United States should indicate that she is prepared to discuss any political or arms-control proposals that the Chinese desire to advance, and simultaneously to discuss the implementation of a declaration against the use of force and China's adherence to the nuclear test ban treaty. The United States should stress that the Warsaw forum provides an adequate means of discussing these issues (and of arriving at agreement if there is political will on both sides to do so), and that it does not seem to the American Government that there is need for any more general Asian political conferences unless China gives better and greater indication of her desire to settle the issues at hand.

There remains the possibility of limited arms-control agreements between the United States, China, and, perhaps, other Asian and non-Asian states, which would contribute to stability within the area. The pressures to create a nuclear-weapon–free zone are likely to grow as China develops her nuclear capability and should not necessarily be resisted by the United States. In fact, the United States may well want to propose a ban on nuclear weapons from a sizable area on both sides of the Chinese border—which would render a surprise Chinese Communist offensive nuclear attack virtually impossible. But the United States should insist that such an agreement must provide for adequate inspection procedures, something the Chinese are unlikely to accept. Whether or not they propose an atom-free zone, the Chinese are likely to press for a general disarmament conference and a general treaty on nuclear disarmament. There would be every reason for the United States to ignore these suggestions, simply pointing out that until China is willing to take more basic steps—

such as renouncing the use of force in the Taiwan Straits and signing the test ban treaty—there seems little point in discussing the possibility of general disarmament with her. The United States might also point out the continued difficulty of negotiating with the Soviet Union on such an issue. Although China certainly must be included at some point in a general disarmament treaty, Soviet agreement is a prime condition, and until it is a real possibility, there is little reason to begin serious negotiations with China.

7

A Major Chinese
Nuclear Capability

THERE IS NO SHARP LINE DIVID-
ing a minor Chinese nuclear capability from a major one,
for most of the problems will remain the same and the policies
to be pursued by China's adversaries will be similar. The dis-
tinguishing factor of a major capability is that with it, Peking will at least appear able directly to attack the United
States. The Soviet ability to threaten the United States directly affected American relations with her European allies,
and the Chinese capability certainly will affect Asian politics.
However, the time when China will have a major nuclear
force is far in the future, and other political, economic, and
technical events will occur in the meantime; it is therefore
difficult to say very much in detail about the dimensions of
an increased Chinese threat and the United States' possible
response to it.

As Chinese nuclear capability grows, the Chinese ability to attack targets closer to China will increase. A fundamental change will occur when the Chinese acquire a hydrogen bomb capability, for this means that any single bomber or missile which reaches its target will do much greater damage than one with atomic weapons only. How soon the Chinese threat becomes more serious will depend in part on the speed of China's weapons development program, and on the emphasis they have and will put on the switch from fission to fission-fusion weapons. Their ability to threaten their neighbors will also depend on how much they emphasize the development of sophisticated delivery systems to penetrate Western defenses. The development of the Chinese capability must also be seen relative to Western technical innovations in air defense and missile defense systems, and to the willingness of Asian states to permit defensive systems manned by U.S. forces on their territory (and, perhaps, to cooperate in installing a regional early-warning system).

It is equally impossible to estimate how soon the developing Chinese capability will pose a direct threat to the United States. This will depend not only on what priority the Chinese give their nuclear program but on how much they will concentrate on building a regional rather than an intercontinental capability. The Chinese, like the Soviets, may decide to concentrate on a capability to inflict nuclear damage on their immediate neighbors, on the grounds that it is a cheaper and more efficient way of deterring an American attack. In this case, and in view of the high costs and resources that would be needed to create an intercontinental delivery capability (either in airplanes that could penetrate American air defenses or in accurate missiles), the Chinese might decide to postpone indefinitely the development of an intercontinental capability.

China's decision will be influenced not only by her estimate of the cost of an intercontinental program but also by whether

her national objectives are thought to require the ability to attack the United States directly, as opposed to an increase in the military potential against her Asian neighbors. In addition, American efforts will substantially affect the cost and effectiveness of any Chinese intercontinental program: Technologically, further American efforts in defense against airplanes and the deployment of an American anti-ballistic missile (ABM) system may be critical in determining how much the Chinese would have to spend to develop a capability to attack American territory. Indeed, the possibility that China could make such an attack may in the long run be the most important argument in favor of the deployment of an American ABM system.

Apparently no ABM system that could now be devised will give the United States a significant advantage over the Soviet Union, and any ABM system would be very expensive. That is to say, it appears that the Russians could, with much less expenditure, build missiles which could destroy any American ABM system currently available or liable to be developed within the coming decade. But this would not hold true against the much cruder missiles the Chinese might be able to develop. It is important to emphasize here that the American Nike-Zeus missile can shoot down a single incoming missile. The decision not to go into full production of the Nike-Zeus was based on the estimate that, before it was produced and deployed, the Soviets would be able to design a missile that would destroy its effectiveness. In general, American decisions on ABM production have been based on considerations of the Soviet threat. It would be premature at this point to install an ABM system against the Chinese intercontinental threat, which is certainly far into the future, but the United States is committed to continued research and development on ABM systems and may at some point decide to deploy one that could destroy most, if not all, of an incoming Chinese missile salvo, even though it did not have the sophistication to deal with Soviet missiles.[1]

Another factor will help to determine whether it is profitable for the Chinese to build an intercontinental strategic system, and that is how large and of what quality the American strategic force is at the time. If the American Government goes ahead with its programs to build a force of intercontinental missiles numbering in the thousands—including hardened Minutemen, mobile Polaris submarines, and, presumably, other systems—it will be very clear to the Chinese that they cannot hope to match it in any way or destroy even a significant part of it in a first strike. It will also be clear that any force China develops is extremely vulnerable to an American first strike, since the great numbers of American missiles permit the multiple targeting necessary to destroy hardened strategic forces. On the other hand, should the United States, on the basis of either a formal disarmament agreement or a more tacit arms-control bargaining with the Soviet Union, decide to build only a small strategic force numbering in the hundreds, China's reasoning can be very different. Against an opponent with only a relatively small number of missiles, the Chinese could hope to develop a force with sufficient second-strike potency to deter attack and that also might appear to be of use in a first-strike situation. This point about Chinese incentives cannot by itself settle the question of whether the United States should build a missile force in the thousands or in the hundreds, but it is a point that will gain considerable importance if and when the Chinese are on the verge of creating an intercontinental strategic system. As in the case of ABM's, it will be necessary for the United States to begin considering her much less sophisticated and poorer Chinese

1 Similarly, if a French, British, or European nuclear program proceeds into the late 1960's or early 1970's, the Soviet Union may decide to deploy large numbers of ABM's against European missiles, while recognizing that it could not be effective against the large number and greater sophistication of American ICBM's.

opponent, as well as the Soviet Union, in making strategic decisions.

In general, the United States tends to underestimate the ability of her opponents, both politically and technologically. Thus, she assumed that the Soviet Union's development of an atomic bomb would occur much later than it in fact did. She was surprised again by the rapid creation of Soviet fission-fusion weapons and perhaps even more surprised when the Soviet Union developed a commanding lead in intercontinental ballistic missiles development and demonstrated heavy-lift capability. Similarly, American officials tended to predict that the Chinese Communists would not capture all of China and that even if they did so, they would become mere puppets of the Soviet Union, unable to control China successfully or to start it on the road toward industrialization. Perhaps in reaction to these past predictions, American officials have more recently tended to overestimate China's industrial and scientific capability.

These overestimates have led American analysts and American policy-makers to begin thinking of China as already a great power in military, political, or economic terms, and to predict the development of a significant Chinese military capability far sooner than is likely. Given the paucity of data about developments in China, it is difficult to be at all precise about predictions of this sort, particularly since they involve so many uncertainties, including China's decisions about the priorities they should give their nuclear delivery programs. Nevertheless, it would seem that the development of any serious Chinese *intercontinental* nuclear capability is unlikely before the 1980's. This does not mean that it is too soon to begin thinking about it: If steps are going to be taken to off-set Chinese power, they should be taken now. Political decisions concerning relations with countries in Asia, as well as military decisions on the development of defensive and offensive strategic forces, should, in fact, be made with the future possibility of a Chinese intercontinental capability in mind. The lead time in changing political attitudes and decisions and in developing weapon systems makes it necessary to think about the early 1970's now and desirable to think about problems of the 1980's. It goes almost without saying that current analysis of the dangers of the 1980's must be flexible enough to accommodate unforeseen political, economic, technological, or ideological changes that may occur before that time is reached.

In trying, then, to come to grips with the difference the development of a Chinese intercontinental capability could make for international politics in the Pacific area, it is necessary to consider, first, the direct threat posed to the United States and, second, the implications it would have for the problems of direct defense against Chinese aggression. What the Chinese are likely to have is a force that in either a first or a second strike could kill millions of Americans. A Chinese first strike is improbable, however, for even "major" capability will not give China nuclear parity with the United States in the twentieth century. Since the Chinese force will be too small for a first strike against the United States, there will be no pressure to pre-empt such an attack at any cost. Conversely, China's capacity to cause millions of American deaths, even though herself obliterated, would be an incentive for the United States *not* to pre-empt gratuitously. One cannot rule out the possibility of the emergence within China of a ruler who attempts on the basis of a modest nuclear force to employ nuclear blackmail against the United States. But the coming to power of such a ruler seems unlikely, and it is difficult to say in advance how one would deal with someone so unbalanced.

The real problem for American foreign policy will be how to maintain the Asian nations' morale and their willingness to oppose Chinese expansion. The problems the United States began to encounter in the mid- and late 1950's and early

1960's within the NATO alliance are likely to develop in a somewhat similar form as China acquires the capability to attack the United States. Asian states will begin to ask themselves whether the defense of Assam or of Burma or even perhaps of Japan is worth the risk to the United States of unspecified millions of casualties. The United States will face the problem that she now faces in Europe—of convincing her allies that she is prepared to come to their defense despite the fact that the fighting might explode into a war involving attacks on American territory. The United States should, while arguing that the Soviet Union will not intervene, make it clear that this threat has always been implicit in the possibility of Soviet involvement in a Sino-American war. The United States should point out that when she came to the aid of the South Koreans, when she aided Chinese Nationalists in the Taiwan Straits, when she intervened in Indochina, and if and where she intervenes in the coming decades, that she did so with some finite possibility that the war might lead to attacks on American territory; the existence of a Chinese intercontinental capability increases very little if at all the over-all possibility of general nuclear war.

The United States will nevertheless want to emphasize that her intercontinental nuclear capability is no substitute for an effective, direct defense strategy for the nations of Asia. As she did in the case of the Soviet threat to Europe, the United States will need to urge even more than it has in the past the development of a full range of options designed to meet any Chinese threat—from subversion through conventional war to tactical nuclear war up to the strategic use of nuclear weapons. As the Chinese develop a major nuclear capability, it will probably be necessary for the United States substantially to augment its Pacific nuclear forces, particularly in anti-aircraft and anti-missile defenses. It will be necessary, however, to recognize that in Asia the fear of even a very small number of Chinese weapons getting through these defenses will become more acute as the probability of their being used rises and as the number of deaths that would result from a single bomb substantially increases. American policy will be a most important message to the Chinese Communists of American determination to defend the countries of Asia despite this growing threat. But it may be desirable at some point to enter into formal guaranties, as the countries of Asia become progressively more desirous of such alliances.

Another major if not dominant factor in the threat a major Chinese nuclear capability could pose is the state of Sino-Soviet relations. If the relationship continues to deteriorate, a Chinese intercontinental nuclear capability will pose a military threat to the Soviet Union as well as to the United States. If the clashes that occurred in the early 1960's on the Sino-Soviet border continue, both the Chinese and the Russians may reach the point where their nuclear capabilities are designed partly, and perhaps in the Chinese case mainly, for deterrence against the other. Possibly, the Chinese will place their missile sites close to the Soviet border rather than close to their southern borders—a posture of clear deterrence against the Soviet Union. Certainly, if the relationship continues to deteriorate, the Chinese would quite justifiably fear the possibility of not only Soviet military moves on the border but also of a Soviet attempt to effect a change in the government in Peking by a combination of military threats and political maneuvers. In these circumstances, a nuclear capability might appear important to the Chinese as a way of deterring the Soviets rather than as a means of dealing with their other neighbors. It may well be that the United States can rely on the Soviet Union in these circumstances to deter any Chinese use of nuclear weapons. The Soviets may make it clear to the Chinese that they would intervene in the event of Chinese use of nuclear weapons, and the Chinese may find this threat more credible from the Russians than from the United States.

At the other extreme, a cementing of the Sino-Soviet alliance might come—at the price of Soviet nuclear aid to the Peking regime. In this case, the Chinese would have a much more sophisticated nuclear capability: Chinese missiles could be as advanced as Soviet missiles, with the decoys necessary to evade an American air defense system and with methods of protection sufficient to deter an American first strike.

It is difficult to predict whether either of these extremes, or a continuation of the current state of Sino-Soviet relations, is more likely, but it is necessary to emphasize that the comments made here are predicated on the assumption of a continuation of the Sino-Soviet dispute but no direct Soviet-Chinese military confrontation.

As the Chinese nuclear capability grows, and as the Chinese stock of fissional material increases, the possibility of the Chinese sharing nuclear weapons with other countries also cannot be ruled out. China may be as reluctant as other nuclear powers have been to turn over to other countries part of her nuclear stockpile, but she may *not* be—particularly in relation to countries far from her borders, as, for example, the nations of Latin America, the Middle East, or Africa. The Chinese may well be willing to establish their great-power status by making nuclear weapons available to revolutionary regimes that have sided with the Chinese in the Sino-Soviet dispute. This possibility, which cannot be excluded, would enormously complicate the containment of localized violence. But the mere threat to turn over nuclear weapons or even to send nuclear-armed volunteers would enhance China's claim to great-power status and her right to be heard at international conferences on issues involving any one of these continents. Any Chinese tendency in this direction will, of course, bring a sharp reaction from the United States and, hopefully, from the Soviet Union, and will underline the problem of preventing the nations of Asia, Africa, and Latin America from accepting Chinese nuclear weapons. Success is likely to come only as part of a more general policy designed to avoid violence in the underdeveloped areas and to promote the peaceful settlement of disputes. However, current trends suggest that violence is likely to continue, and the temptation of local powers to accept the offer of Chinese nuclear weapons or at least of a Chinese "nuclear umbrella" may prove great. In such circumstances, the United States will probably want to attempt, either alone or with the Soviet Union, a blockade of China to prevent her from shipping nuclear weapons to other countries. The fact that the Chinese were prepared to share nuclear weapons with unstable regimes in other areas might induce the kind of Soviet-American cooperation sufficient to contain and perhaps eliminate Chinese nuclear power.

Long-run estimates of the dangers of a Chinese nuclear capability bear out the prediction that the further spread of nuclear weapons is likely to increase instability in the world. The extent to which a Chinese nuclear capability will lessen stability depends on political developments within China, China's relations with her neighbors and with the United States and the Soviet Union. Surely, however, not all the disputes in Asia will be resolved within this century. In the long run, a China armed with nuclear weapons will significantly complicate the problems of American foreign policy in the Far East and throughout the world.

Index

163

Publications Written under the Auspices of the Center for International Affairs Harvard University

Created in 1958, the Center for International Affairs fosters advanced study of basic world problems by scholars from various disciplines and senior officials from many countries. The research at the Center focuses on economic and social development, the management of force in the modern world, and the evolving roles of Western Europe and the Communist bloc. The published results appear here in the order in which they have been issued. The research programs are supervised by Professors Robert R. Bowie (Director of the Center), Samuel P. Huntington, Alex Inkeles, Henry A. Kissinger, Edward S. Mason, Thomas C. Schelling, and Raymond Vernon.

BOOKS

The Soviet Bloc, by Zbigniew K. Brzezinski, 1960 (jointly with the Russian Research Center). Harvard University Press.

The Necessity for Choice, by Henry A. Kissinger, 1961. Harper & Bros.

Strategy and Arms Control, by Thomas C. Schelling and Morton H. Halperin, 1961. Twentieth Century Fund.

Rift and Revolt in Hungary, by Ferenc A. Váli, 1961. Harvard University Press.

United States Manufacturing Investment in Brazil, by Lincoln Gordon and Engelbert L. Grommers, 1962. Harvard Business School.

The Economy of Cyprus, by A. J. Meyer, with Simos Vassiliou,

1962 (jointly with the Center for Middle Eastern Studies). Harvard University Press.

Entrepreneurs of Lebanon, by Yusif A. Sayigh, 1962 (jointly with the Center for Middle Eastern Studies). Harvard University Press.

Communist China 1955–1959: Policy Documents with Analysis, with a Foreword by Robert R. Bowie and John K. Fairbank, 1962 (jointly with the East Asian Research Center). Harvard University Press.

In Search of France, by Stanley Hoffmann, Charles P. Kindleberger, Laurence Wylie, Jesse R. Pitts, Jean-Baptiste Duroselle, and François Goguel, 1963. Harvard University Press.

Somali Nationalism, by Saadia Touval, 1963. Harvard University Press.

The Dilemma of Mexico's Development, by Raymond Vernon, 1963. Harvard University Press.

Limited War in the Nuclear Age, by Morton H. Halperin, 1963. John Wiley & Sons.

The Arms Debate, by Robert A. Levine, 1963. Harvard University Press.

Africans on the Land, by Montague Yudelman, 1964. Harvard University Press.

Counterinsurgency Warfare, by David Galula, 1964. Frederick A. Praeger, Inc.

People and Policy in the Middle East, by Max Weston Thornburg, 1964. W. W. Norton & Co.

Shaping the Future, by Robert R. Bowie, 1964. Columbia University Press.

Foreign Aid and Foreign Policy, by Edward S. Mason (jointly with the Council on Foreign Relations), 1964. Harper & Row.

Public Policy and Private Enterprise in Mexico, by M. S. Wionczek, D. H. Shelton, C. P. Blair, and R. Izquierdo, ed. Raymond Vernon, 1964. Harvard University Press.

How Nations Negotiate, by Fred Iklé, 1964. Harper & Row.

China and the Bomb, by Morton H. Halperin, 1965. Frederick A. Praeger, Inc.

Democracy in Germany (Jodidi Lectures), by Fritz Erler, 1965. Harvard University Press.

OCCASIONAL PAPERS, PUBLISHED BY THE CENTER FOR INTERNATIONAL AFFAIRS

1. *A Plan for Planning: The Need for a Better Method of Assisting Underdeveloped Countries on Their Economic Policies,* by Gustav F. Papanek, 1961.
2. *The Flow of Resources from Rich to Poor,* by Alan D. Neale, 1961.
3. *Limited War: An Essay on the Development of the Theory and an Annotated Bibliography,* by Morton H. Halperin, 1962.
4. *Reflections on the Failure of the First West Indian Federation,* by Hugh W. Springer, 1962.
5. *On the Interaction of Opposing Forces under Possible Arms Agreements,* by Glenn A. Kent, 1963.
6. *Europe's Northern Cap and the Soviet Union,* by Nils Örvik, 1963.
7. *Civil Administration in the Punjab: An Analysis of a State Government in India,* by E. N. Nangat Rai, 1963.
8. *On the Appropriate Size of a Development Program,* by Edward S. Mason, 1964.
9. *Self-determination Revisited in the Era of Decolonization,* by Rupert Emerson, 1964.
10. *The Planning and Execution of Economic Development in Southeast Asia,* by Clair Wilcox, 1965.

Publications Written under the Auspices of the East Asian Research Center Harvard University
(Published by Harvard University Press)

12. *China and the Helping Hand, 1938–1945,* by Arthur N. Young, 1963.
13. *Research Guide to the May Fourth Movement: Intellectual Revolution in Modern China, 1915–1924,* by Chow Tse-tsung, 1963.
14. *The United States and the Far Eastern Crisis of 1933–1938 (from the Manchurian Incident through the Initial Stage of the Undeclared Sino-Japanese War),* by Dorothy Borg, 1964.
15. *China and the West, 1858–1861: The Origins of the Tsungli Yamen,* by Masataka Banno, 1964.
16. *In Search of Wealth and Power: Yen Fu and the West,* by Benjamin Schwartz, 1964.
17. *The Origins of Entrepreneurship in Meiji Japan,* by Johannes Hirschmeier (S.V.D.), 1964.
18. *Commissioner Lin and the Opium War,* by Chang Hsin-pao, 1964.